Praise for Faith on the Streets

'Les's dedication and the commitment of the Street Pastors to their communities are an inspiration to many. More importantly he shows that real results can be achieved through genuine partnership.'

Peter O'Brien, Corporate Relations Director,
Diageo Western Europe.

'At the time when I was a Home Office Minister, I saw at first-hand how street pastors made a valuable contribution to keeping our streets safe. A real example of faith in action.'

Vernon Coaker, MP.

'Street Pastors are the embodiment of Citizens in Policing – they are people making a difference in their community and this book is a very welcome insight.'

Rob Beckley, Chief Operating Officer, College of Policing.

'The flourishing of Street Pastors over 10 years, which has been a blessing to so many, has at its source a core vision held by Les Isaac and those who have worked with him of the importance of resilient community partnerships undergirded by strong Christian faith. Read on and give thanks!'

Christopher Chessun, Bishop of Southwark.

Faith on the Streets

Christians in action through the Street Pastors movement

LES ISAAC AND ROSALIND DAVIES

HODDER

First published in Great Britain in 2014 by Hodder & Stoughton
An Hachette UK company

This paperback edition first published in 2015

1

A CIP catalogue record for this title is available from the British Library

ISBN 978 1 444 75010 2
eBook ISBN 978 1 444 75011 9

Typeset in Chaparral Pro by Palimpsest Book Production Ltd,
Falkirk, Stirlingshire

Printed and bound by CPI Group (UK) Ltd, Croydon, CR0 4YY

Hodder & Stoughton policy is to use papers that are natural, renewable
and recyclable products and made from wood grown in sustainable
forests. The logging and manufacturing processes are expected to
conform to the environmental regulations of the country of origin.

Hodder & Stoughton Ltd
Carmelite House
50 Victoria Embankment
London EC4Y 0DZ

www.hodderfaith.com

Contents

Acknowledgements

At the heart of this book are many people who work together to bring change. They are young and old, living in villages and cities, belonging to different church denominations, and they come together through Street Pastors for the greater good of society. We want to acknowledge all of them. There is so much good news they could tell us that we haven't yet heard or been able to record here.

We would like to express our thanks to the many generous individuals who have contributed to this book and whose commitment to being a disciple of Jesus Christ and disseminating the values of Street Pastors has inspired deep thinking and loving engagement with the places where they live. It has been a great privilege to learn from you. We are grateful to Adrian Prior Sankey, Anne Fothergill, Aran Richardson, Chris Roe, Gary Smith, James Mackenzie, Joy Liddle, Judith Allen, June Clarke, Kathy Howe, Les Tuckwell, Mandy Harding, Mark Hadfield, Mark Tomlinson, Monica Abdala, Neil Charlton, Penny Roe, Richard Pitt, Roger Ede, Ros Ede, Roy Smeeth, Sam Douthwaite, Sarah Gray, Sharon Constance, Stuart Clarke and Yvonne Norris.

The book is greatly enriched by the willingness of four individuals to tell the story of the night that they came into contact with street pastors. Thank you to James, Sandy, Joanne and Christi. A crowd of Twitter users has been kind enough to give permission for their tweets about Street Pastors to be used; your user names are recorded in the pages that follow.

All the staff at Ascension Trust have been patient with the book-writing process and diligent in helping with research.

Particular thanks are due to Andrew MacKay, Christine Bongo, Eustace Constance and Martin Pointing.

For their efficient recall, and for all they have contributed to the Street Pastors movement, we would like to thank Bobby Wilmot, Roger Forster and Simon Thomas. The Christian Police Association (CPA) has greatly assisted us in building up a picture of the Metropolitan Police's role in the launch of Street Pastors and in the relations between the police and churches in the 1990s and 2000s. We are also grateful to the office of the Police Service Citizens in Policing Portfolio and Rob Beckley, Chief Operating Officer for the College of Policing, as well as Bob Pull, Don Axcell, Nick Cornish, Paul Hill, DC Andy Coles, PC Phil Skedgell, Sergeant Gary Watts and Inspector Roger Bartlett.

Thank you also to the office of David Burrowes MP, the Mayor of Lewisham, Sir Steve Bullock, David Farmer at Plymstock School, Elizabeth Sims at Archbishop Tenison School, Ruth Evans at Cantell Maths and Computing College and Matt Bird of the Cinnamon Network.

The welcome we have received at Hodder Faith has been much appreciated. Thank you, Ian Metcalfe and Katherine Venn. Richard Herkes, editorial consultant, was a great source of advice and insight in the early stages of the project.

Knowing that I am loved and supported by my family is very special to me. Their encouragement and especially the support of my wife, Louise, through all the years of my work, means so much.

Les Isaac

My lovely family supplies me with distractions, questions, insight, solutions, optimism and encouragement. Thank you, Graham, Eleanor, Ben and Matthew.

Rosalind Davies

Preface

It is extraordinary. In just ten years, Street Pastors has gone from a novel idea, to a pioneering initiative, to an indispensable ministry celebrated across society. It's an extraordinary story, but then, Les Isaac and the street pastors are extraordinary, and Christians worship an extraordinary God.

When Jesus tells the story of the Good Samaritan, it is not a story about the 'why?' of social action. It is a story of a man who sees a need, rolls up his sleeves, and helps, regardless of the risks and costs. But above all, what is so surprising in Jesus' story is that it was a Samaritan, who came from a different world from the Jewish traveller, who stepped in to help this stranger. Street pastors are modern-day Good Samaritans in just this way. They step out to help those who are geographically nearby, even if they are otherwise in different worlds.

One remarkable sign of Street Pastors' success is the recognition they have received in Parliament. MPs can be suspicious of faith-based initiatives, but praise for Street Pastors has been effusive. Not only has Les passed on his enthusiasm to Street Pastors volunteers, but politicians, police and community authorities have caught the vision of what they are working to do.

Not long ago, the idea of a faith-based ministry, enacted solely by highly motivated volunteers, having a huge impact all across the UK, would have been thought improbable and unworkable. People would have said that volunteers were too unreliable. Others would have said that faith-based ministries proselytise and divide. Still others would have worried that local volunteers would have been helplessly out of their depth in all but exceptional cases.

Street Pastors has exploded these beliefs. It turns out that the potential in our communities is so much greater than many believed, and that hundreds of church communities up and down the country are packed with people passionate about serving their communities. The impact of Street Pastors has not only been in their local communities, but in the way that society sees voluntary work. It may not be news for some of us, but for many, Street Pastors has redefined the whole debate. At all levels of local and national politics and public service, the work of passionate, talented, local volunteers is once again being held up as indispensable to building strong, safe, thriving communities.

As Street Pastors continues to develop and grow, we come back to the parable of the Good Samaritan. The Samaritan served and helped in the ways he best could, but when others were better placed to help the injured traveller, the Samaritan took him to them. The Samaritan could not provide rest and care for the traveller to recuperate, but he made sure that a local innkeeper could properly take care of him, and carefully passed on the responsibility for the man. As Street Pastors continues, building the relationships with those who can serve in other ways – the police and local authorities – is a key step.

In the recent 'Faith in the Community' report by Christians in Parliament and the Evangelical Alliance (June 2013), which I was delighted to be involved in, the Archbishop of York put it well. He said,

Building strong working relationships between local authorities and religious communities should not be based on mere 'tolerance'. It should be about talking, listening, and growing together. Together, working in unity of spirit, we are stronger than when we try to do things in isolation.

There will still be those who wish to sideline the work done by faith-based groups, but they remain wrong and that is becoming increasingly accepted. There are many challenges as these groups and volunteers seek to integrate their work with that of government and other volunteer organisations. Yet the expertise, the will and the passion of groups like Street Pastors means I am confident that these bonds will only strengthen over time, and communities across the country will be immensely richer for it.

This book is a testament to that expertise, that will and that passion. Les Isaac and all those involved with this movement have shown a truly Christ-like example. They display an attitude that does not defensively ask 'Who is my neighbour?' but that, seeing a need, seeks to listen, to care and to help.

David Burrowes, Patron of Street Pastors
MP for Enfield Southgate
August 2013

Introduction

by Rosalind Davies

....

Connections

A couple of years after Street Pastors was first established, I was invited to observe one of the London teams in action. It was a warm summer night but I still had to wear the Street Pastors Observer jacket and the regulation cap. The streets were full of people; it was just like daytime, in fact. I remember thinking that the crowds around me hadn't 'gone out' for the evening in the way that I understood it. It seemed to me that they were just going about their business – it was just that it happened to be late at night. Music was playing, babies were being pushed in pushchairs, old men and women chatted as they sat on chairs brought out from houses. Groups of youngsters called to each other, making arrangements to meet later. To them it was not late: 'later' was still an option. I saw a christening party spill out onto the street. On the main roads, cars and buses negotiated people who couldn't stay on the pavements. Nightclubs were busy as well as cafés and takeaways, all of them with a cluster of people on the threshold, heading in or coming out.

I felt ill at ease. I wanted to catch the eye of a passer-by and call out my greeting, like the rest of the team were doing, but I was distracted by the sights and sounds and by negotiating my way along the pavement. I was making a bad job of the infamous 'street pastors' walk', the slow amble that communicates approachability and availability. This new world contained a sensory overload. I met the girl who was barely clothed; I heard the raucous stag night; I saw the anguished teenager who couldn't find her mates; the serviceman leaving for a tour of duty the next day; the wife, the wife's ex and the wife's new partner; the group dressed up in Elvis costumes; the rough sleeper; the incapable fifteen-year-old; the student high on drugs; the man for whom Saturday night is always about escapism. Street pastors make it their business to learn about this after-hours culture. They don't run away. They draw close to people in what are often messy, ugly situations.

I knew there was naivety written all over my face as I scurried through Brixton that night, getting a glimpse of a blunt alternative to the routines of my own life. What I had seen of this place in daylight was only half the picture.

Not everywhere that street pastors walk will be like this part of the capital on a Friday or Saturday night but, whatever the setting, all street pastors must acclimatise to the way that life is carried on – often with emotions heightened by alcohol and drugs – right there under the street lights. There is a sense in which street pastors are profoundly out of place in this landscape. I've sometimes thought about the awkwardness of the pairing: alcohol-fuelled aggression and a street pastors' offer of a lollipop; the loud excesses of a celebration and a street pastor stooping to sweep broken glass into a dustpan. Where there is noise, laughter, tears, fights, anger, friendship, camaraderie, is there any room for a stranger, I wonder? Emotions are amplified, they are let rip. It would be easy to think that these people on their night out are in charge, that they have staked their claim and the streets are theirs. So it would be easy also to play it safe, keep a distance and leave the roads clear for the police and the ambulances.

My naivety that night in Brixton was real, as was the fear I felt, faced by this scene of anarchy. But street pastors don't deal in naivety or fear. Street pastors get informed, they get trained, they get real and they get involved. I believe that getting involved in lives outside of our own circle of family and friendship is one of life's fundamental challenges: it's not always natural to do it. Sometimes I aspire to it, but I'm not sure how to show it, how to demonstrate it. I've heard a police officer joke about the perils of narrow-mindedness as he told of a period of unrest and rioting in a city on the south coast some years ago. In the middle of the disturbances, he went to a public meeting, where the most talked about item on the agenda was cycling on the pavements.

When the Street Pastors initiative was still on the drawing board in 2002, church and community leaders from Jamaica took part in public meetings in London and other major cities in this country. One of their key messages was the importance of involvement in difficult, depressed or dangerous neighbourhoods, and they warned audiences about the way that locals in the uptown neighbourhoods of Kingston, Jamaica, had retreated from the problems of guns and gang violence in Trench Town, the downtown district of their city. Grille-makers and iron-mongers did great business. The uptown residents were scared of the other world around the corner, and did not want to know anything more about it. The two societies became segregated.

The message from the Jamaican leaders was that the understandable desire to stay on the sidelines and to ignore difficult situations can lead to further fear and segregation. When, through a campaign led by churches, residents who had left Trench Town thirty years previously (and sworn they would never go back) were persuaded to set foot in the district once more, they began to understand what they could not learn from watching the TV news. They realised that if they could get out of their car and stand among the bullet-scarred houses, it might be possible for their involvement to grow. They broke through the barrier that 'the unknown' had erected and made a small first step. 'Come and see' was the invitation from the church and community leaders in Kingston, and 'going' and 'seeing'

3

made the difference between ignorance and fear and information and hope.

Many of those who have contributed to the content of this
book are firm believers in the power of information leading to
involvement. Knowledge comes when we get out and explore
the wider community in which we live. That might often mean
going into places that we're not so familiar or comfortable with:
perhaps the nearby estate, a council chamber, the high street
at night or a residents' association meeting. One passionate
advocate of this concerned interaction describes the process of
moving from 'naive compassion' to 'informed compassion', the
process that takes place when we get a better picture of what
is going on in our towns or cities.

Those who volunteer to be street pastors are people who have
realised the power and the eloquence of human contact in places
where you might least expect it. These are people who believe
that humans are more alike than they are different; they have
an innate confidence in the seed of connection between them
and another person, which in turn gives them the humility and
the boldness to pause in the middle of a raucous crowd to chat,
comfort – or to get the dustpan out. Four individuals who have
experienced help, care and interest from a street pastor were
generous enough to share their stories in this book. You can
read James's story in Chapter 2, Sandy's in Chapter 5, Joanne's
in Chapter 8 and Christi's in Chapter 11. For some of the 'users'
of Street Pastors, the connection was sudden and timely; for
others it was a rapport built over the long term based on a
street pastor giving them a listening ear and the freedom to
question.

As street pastors themselves report, there is a great deal of
variety in the work done under the Street Pastors banner of
'Caring, listening and helping'. Chapter 1 looks in more detail
at the role and responsibilities of a street pastor. For some
volunteers it might involve handing a knife in at a police station,

helping a schoolchild who has just had her phone stolen or bringing calm during times of riot or disturbance. For others it means setting up a 'safe space' on the front path of a church, picking up litter or chatting to nightclub door staff. Incidents and encounters from all points along this range are mentioned in this book. There are approximately 10,000 trained Street Pastors volunteers in the UK, who are serving their towns and cities, schools, parks and shopping centres across more than 270 locations in the UK. While the majority of them operate during the drink-fuelled hours of the night, others function in different contexts, at whatever time of day they are most needed. This book investigates what exactly is being offered in those hours and what is valuable about a Christian-led group of volunteers playing a part in the infrastructure of public life.

Collective consciousness

The one-to-one connection is a starting point; this book also shows how bridges are being built between different sections of community. Teams of street pastors are key to this process: they are accepted as mediators with an independent voice. They also see this bridge-building taking place as they work in partnership with the police and local government. The Street Pastors movement has brought divergent worlds together – the Church, the police and the local authority – through the clash of institutional systems and methodologies into civic partnership. This book seeks to contribute to the debate about the place of faith groups in public life, a topic that has been brought particularly into focus in these years of austerity and budget cuts. Chapters 6 and 7 specifically examine the journey towards effective partnership between the stakeholders in our towns and cities. Changes in the Church as an institution, as part of the civic landscape, are the subject of Chapter 9. As street pastors represent the Church, and as they take 'Church' out of the four walls of a building, we are seeing a repositioning of Christian activity on a bigger scale than ever before. The chapter looks at the informal spiritual engagement that takes place around street pastors on their patrols among people who have no connection to mainstream Church. In this sense 'Church' is moving away from being a 'destination' for a Sunday morning to being the expression of biblical principles through the movement of individual Christians *out* from the hub (the Church) and *into* the surroundings, made visible through the practical demonstration of God's love.

Two of the individuals who have generously shared their stories of the night they met a street pastor, explain how a longer-term relationship with Christians and churches was something they wanted to pursue. Talking about the faith that motivates them is something that comes naturally, on occasions, to a street pastor during the course of his or her work, and when an individual's meeting with a street pastor sparks or coincides with that person's spiritual journey, we all give the glory to God. 'We do not present ourselves as people with our heads in heaven,' Les Isaac, founder of Street Pastors, said in an early press interview. 'Though Christians are indeed heavenly minded, I believe that they have an earthly use!' The Church's connection to the real world and the problems of twenty-first-century society is made real when Christians are prepared to put their money where their mouths are. Anyone involved in charitable enterprise, whether that is as a sponsor, volunteer or manager, will recognise this call to stop 'talking' and start 'walking'.

As I've observed the Street Pastors movement over the last ten years, I've seen what can happen when one person breaks the mould that says 'you stay in your corner, I'll stay in mine'. Taking care of the place where we live and our neighbours is an attitude that has the potential to be contagious. An incident of low-level vandalism in the town of Tiverton in mid-Devon is one such example. Here, one evening, patrolling street pastors saw a group of lads pulling up plants on the grass verge. Walking over to the boys, the team encouraged them to replant the flowers. After a few minutes a group of girls appeared on the scene. 'What are you doing talking to those boys?' they asked. 'We'll stay here to look out for you.'

It's a story of small gestures but at the same time it expresses connections between people: adults talking to teenagers; strangers encouraging others to restore rather than destroy; a group of young girls acting protectively towards adults. The first connection between the street pastors and the boys sparks the second one between the girls and the street pastors. This book tells of the ways that street pastors are acting as bridge-builders in our society, forming links between different parts of communities.

This book examines how certain individuals are committed to playing their part in building healthy communities. Such people show us that a shared responsibility for a healthy society can be expressed through these collaborations as we value and sustain each other. I am thinking, for example, of one outlet of a well-known burger restaurant chain that, when street pastors ask for help, has allowed stranded or vulnerable young women to sleep on their premises, under the watchful eye of door staff, until they can make their way home the next day. Street pastors in Newcastle tell of the night they were out on duty and came across a homeless man lying in the snow with no shoes on. As they tended to him and wrapped him in a foil blanket, a young man passing by stopped to see what was going on and offered his new trainers to the homeless man. In London, a group of over-zealous lads rushed to the aid of a street pastor who had had her cap knocked off deliberately by a passer-by. Within seconds the men had the culprit pinned up against the wall, and were asking the street pastor, 'Do you want us to do him?' On a more serious note, a doorman working in the clubs of Stirling says that before street pastors came on the scene, his primary responsibility was to get people who had drunk too much off the premises. Now, no one is thrown out, he says, until he has made contact with street pastors and he knows that they will be moved on safely.

Sometimes headline-grabbing, sometimes simple and understated, the work of street pastors encourages us all to unlock our own isolation from the environment we live in and to look to influence for the better individuals, families and communities. Other worlds are all around us: the world of the rough sleeper, the city centre manager or the schoolchild is close at hand. When street pastors and school pastors care for and listen to another person without prejudice, they are entering that person's world. This vision of shared social responsibility leaves us all contemplating the small things that can make a big difference.

A big picture

This book tells the story of the birth of Street Pastors. The early years of Les Isaac's life and ministry are related in Part 2 (Chapters 3 and 4), and Les describes the core values that he and the other founders of Street Pastors developed. Other innovations that were taking place in the 1990s are also part of this history, such as Adopt-a-Cop, which came into being through officers in the Metropolitan branch of the Christian Police Association, and a new engagement between churches and secular agencies – for example in Manchester, where foundations for a significant expression of cooperation between Christians and statutory bodies were laid. This went on to become the Redeeming Our Communities initiative (ROC).

Volunteers who were part of the first team that took to the streets of Brixton in April 2003 commented afterwards that the thing that stood out most for them that night was how willing people were to talk to them. These pioneering volunteers describe this first patrol in their own words in Chapter 4. There were plenty of people asking who they were and what they were doing; one driver even made a U-turn to call out through his car window, 'Who are you people?' That level of surprise has receded now, but the ethos of Street Pastors always invites curiosity: why has this man given up a night's sleep? Why has this young lady spent an hour sitting with a person covered in vomit? Why have these people left their comfortable homes when the temperature is below zero? Some people recognise the term 'pastor' (others have coined their own versions: street patrols, street pastilles, street pasta, street angels, personal angel, God slots, legends, to name a few), but others will ask what it really means. When they hear the answer, that street pastors are Christians who are offering practical help and demonstrating God's love, there is a high level of understanding of the role and the fact that a 'pastor' is there to help an individual in a time of need.

The trust that has grown in the Street Pastors movement has created a platform for the long-awaited development of School Pastors (see Chapter 10), and for the facilitation of Street Pastors initiatives in a growing number of cities overseas. This international growth, in addition to the UK's 270 independent Street Pastors charities, has made the legal and policy remit at head office a vital element of the network model of operation (see Chapter 12).

Local people know about local tensions, the rivers of mistrust and scepticism, histories of division and territorial thuggery in their towns and cities. Local people – people who know what is expected of them and are able to engage in local relationships and encourage others to be involved – are the basis of the strongest model for the Street Pastors movement. Street pastors are people who know that the problems are massive but that they can be obedient and faithful in the small things, engaging with local issues and feeding their compassion with information and understanding. They are people who trust God to use them in ways they may never know about, and to equip them to be a friend, if only for a short while, to someone in need.

Finding ways to connect with each other and connect with the place where we live is all the more important in our disconnected world, where the appeal of belonging to something bigger than oneself has died for many. How healthy is your desire to connect with people or places? It might be the reason that you get out of bed in the morning. Or it might be something that is a 'task' you feel that you must tick off a list. I know that sometimes I need to slow my step, to interrupt my plans and the linear course I have plotted for the day in order to open my eyes to the other worlds around me. Jesus is the model that I need to follow. Jesus shows me what is good about connecting with people. Others, like Les Isaac, also inspire me. It was Les who drew my attention to a verse in the Old Testament that has been meaningful to me ever since. It's found in the book of Proverbs and goes like this: 'As iron sharpens iron, so one man sharpens another.' These are words about human relations – bite-sized wisdom for friendships everywhere. To me they say, simply, we can be better together than we can be apart. It reminds me that another person can sharpen my focus, encourage me to keep going, inspire me to care for others and deepen my sense of belonging.

....

PART ONE

What is a Street Pastor?

@WadeyLady001

I've just seen Street Pastors on the big bad night-time streets of Catford. Never seen them before. Had to google them

Ready for anything:
The role of a street pastor

....

What is a street pastor?

A street pastor is a volunteer who cares for, listens to and helps other people, particularly in the night-time environment, in busy areas where people are drinking, partying and moving between pubs and clubs. Working in small teams of men and women, they will be in contact with bouncers and door staff, CCTV officers and the police, as an integral part of neighbourhood safety, until the streets start to get quieter, around 4 a.m. A street pastor is someone who is concerned for their community, for vulnerable people and, especially, for young people – more than half the people that the volunteers meet are aged between eighteen and twenty-five years. Volunteers are recognisable on the streets in their Street Pastors jacket and cap and, after they have been trained, most of them go out on patrol on a Friday or Saturday night once every four weeks.

Street pastors are able to respond to situations where a night out has not gone as planned, where there is aggression or antisocial behaviour, or emotions are running high, fuelled by drink or drugs. Street pastors are often involved in the night-time economy in simple, straightforward but important ways, demonstrating the 'soft' skills that free up local policing teams to respond to more serious incidents. For example, street pastors often escort vulnerable people to a taxi rank or a place of safety, wait with a person while they sober up sufficiently to walk, provide water and foil blankets where needed, pick up bottles or broken glass that could be used as a weapon, and give first aid to those with minor injuries. They help people who start the night with a group of friends but later find themselves alone and incapable of getting home safely.

They are a positive, friendly and inclusive presence, and for those who want to chat, they are good listeners. Street pastors are always in touch with a small group of prayer supporters, called 'prayer pastors', who pray that calm will be restored in the incidents that are reported to them by the street pastors over the phone or radio link. In some towns and cities, street pastors have been given responsibilities in the daytime, to be a reassuring presence on patrol in and around schools, in public parks or in shopping centres.

@kleephotography
Street Pastoring for the third consecutive Saturday. I fancy a pint. #streetpastors

A street pastor is someone who is able and willing to build bridges between individuals in times of conflict or need. They can make links between individuals and relevant statutory or voluntary agencies, or between an individual who needs help and an individual who can give help. They will be a person who can approach others in a non-judgemental way, listen to them without forming preconceived ideas and, by helping and caring for others, will be demonstrating the good news of Jesus Christ. Whatever they are doing or saying, they will be an ambassador for Jesus.

Who can be a street pastor?

Street pastors come from right across the Christian community and can be anyone who:

* has a passion for Jesus and the community;
* has been committed to a church fellowship for more than one year, with a personal reference from their minister or church leader;
* has attended the training programme;
* is over the age of eighteen;
* has been checked by the DBS (Disclosure and Barring Service).

Training

Training a new street pastor or refreshing the training of an experienced volunteer is always a priority for Ascension Trust, the umbrella body that governs and administers Street Pastors. The trust always aims to deliver practical training, not academic learning. The training manual that accompanies the training course presents the ethos of the initiative and contains resources to prepare teams for appropriate and relevant relationships on the streets. It brings together the challenges of a Christian responsibility for our neighbourhoods with the practical skills and awareness vital to a street pastor's role.

The training manual contains outlines for eight core areas of training and in addition, builds in some flexibility to the programme, so that each area can choose other subjects that will provide additional training in skills relevant to the needs that they will regularly encounter. For example, some teams have established a training link with agencies like the Samaritans or have called upon the experience of the ambulance service to provide tailored first-aid tuition. Many have found a visit to the CCTV control room or a local hostel useful preparation. Two 'field assignments' are required as part of the training course during which trainees are actively involved in patrols. Ascension Trust recommends that a total of forty-two hours of training in core and elective subjects should be undertaken in the first eighteen months after commissioning. Locally tailored training modules are in addition to the forty-two hours.

Most new volunteers will take part in sessions about understanding Christianity in the context of contemporary culture. Following the Bible's encouragement to always be prepared to give an answer to everyone who asks about the hope that a Christian has (1 Peter 3:15), many areas provide training on 'Giving an account of your hope'. It is designed to help a person analyse their own faith story, and learn how to share it in ways that are adapted to the listener and the context. A good street pastor is able to get his or her own experiences and testimony in order so that they can be shared at a moment's notice.

Early in the training programme, all new volunteers will be part of a session called 'Roles and responsibilities'. This takes a first look at the role of a street pastor and sets out the criteria for continuing with training. It also paints a picture of the kind of person who makes a good street pastor.

A street pastor is . . .

Someone with a genuine interest in people

This means being a person who is not patronising and who is not threatening in their manner. Some Street Pastors teams find that those street pastors who are most easily accepted into tense situations on the street are female and older. It's known as the 'granny factor'. So, analysing this common factor, it's true to say that for all volunteers, male and female, the key to being able to approach a person with genuine interest is to relate to them as a person, not *solely* as a drunk or a rough sleeper or an aggressor. Having a genuine interest in people means being ready to ascribe dignity to an individual. In many cases, this is something that street pastors try to do in practical ways, for example, by making sure a young girl lying on the ground is properly covered up and decent, or by cleaning vomit or blood from a person's face or hair.

@CllrPaul4Cowick
Unidentifiable music from @TimepieceExeter as backing track to work of #StreetPastors looking after *tired and emotional* man vomiting . . .

Someone who can resist making assumptions
A street pastor in training will be challenged to think about how easy it is to make assumptions and judge a person by their appearance or their dialect, perhaps even by their skin colour. A street pastor must resist any inward or outward prejudice, particularly being careful to keep their facial reactions to a minimum, no matter what is shared with them. A street pastor offers non-judgemental support.

Someone who can give the gift of time
A street pastor's job on the streets can often mean that they are moving from one hot spot to the next, or from one group of people to the another. However, a good street pastor gives a person the time that they need to share what they want to share, showing them that they have their full attention. A quiet spell is a good chance to chat to door staff and staff in take-aways or restaurants.

Someone who is patient
Though most people greet street pastors warmly, there are others that react antagonistically or in a flippant or sarcastic way. At times like this, a street pastor will give the conversation

time. There may be something that triggers a dramatic change in the conversation after a while. Street pastors work in many contexts in which it takes time to make sense of what someone is trying to communicate, or in which an individual is not in control of their faculties. Patience is needed from the outset, and it may take a long time to establish the best course of action for that person. Likewise, a street pastor must be prepared for nights when there is a lot of waiting around, for a taxi or a parent to arrive.

Someone who is good at reading body language

A street pastor needs to be able to test the temperature of a conversation and assess whether emotions are cooling down or cranking up. The training course will provide lots of opportunities to think about different kinds of body language and how a street pastor can promote calm by encouraging a volatile individual to speak more slowly or sit down. An experienced street pastor will learn over time, as they meet a wide variety of people on the streets, that not everyone is in party mode. Therefore it is good to have a 'ready for anything' approach.

Someone who is skilled in initiating conversations

One of the best qualities a street pastor can have is the ability to initiate a conversation, and so a street pastor's training may well include some role-playing to help a volunteer develop techniques for initiating and maintaining a conversation. It's a skill to be able to greet someone, exchange a few words, and then draw out another comment or observation from which a more sustained conversation can grow. Where there is hostility or provocation, the ability to keep a conversation going long enough to uncover the questions or feelings behind the antagonism is something many street pastors develop. Similarly, it is sometimes important to discover the question behind the question. It may be that a person doesn't quite know how to ask the question that they really want an answer to, so they dress it up as another question that they think is ask-able or will not raise a laugh among their mates. This may be particularly true of questions that arise from personal experience or anguish.

@Tain_Pastors
Due to be -4° tonight . . . better dig out our fleeces and woolly hats! #Tain #StreetPastors

Prayer pastors

All street pastors know the value of prayer underpinning all that they do, and are supported in prayer by others gathering together (or sometimes alone at home) to pray for them while they are out on the streets. These people are a vital part of a Street Pastors team and are known as prayer pastors; they have a less public role but are nonetheless integral to the work of street pastors. It is very important that when street pastors go out on duty they have a team of people praying for them, and everyone involved in the initiative believes that prayer and action are great partners. These prayer pastors will 'send' them out in prayer, pray for their safety during the evening and prayerfully respond to situations and needs on the streets that are relayed to them over the radio or telephone.

For many Street Pastors teams these praying people will take the form of a small group of dedicated prayer pastors who meet at the Street Pastors base, pray with the team as they prepare to go out and remain at base for the rest of the duty. There are other ways, however, in which street pastors are supported in prayer. There are many individuals who want to pray for the work of their local street pastors but prefer, or need, to pray at home. There may also be one-off local prayer events for Street Pastors or large-scale national initiatives to encourage Christians across the country to pray for their communities and their street pastors. The year 2012 was a Year of Prayer for our streets, during which many prayer ministries, not just Prayer Pastors, joined together to focus on praying for our nation.

Praying through the duration of a patrol, through the night and into the early hours of the morning, is no easy option. Street pastors will feed information on what is happening on the street back to the prayer team via radio or mobile phone, so that times of crisis, conflict or potential flashpoints are covered in prayer, and so that prayer pastors can respond quickly to the needs of members of the public, who sometimes ask for prayer.

@jessielongstaff
In a 4-minute walk I just saw 3 riot vans, 2 police cars, 6 police people, 4 street pastors, 2 gangs complete with dogs, a Rottweiler

Sam Douthwaite, co-ordinator of Newcastle Street Pastors, describes a street pastor's role and the costs and the privileges of serving his community.
Street Pastors have made a significant difference to the night-time economy of Newcastle. Some of our volunteers travel a long distance to do their shift because they feel God's calling to care for the region. The city needs people like this who are willing to respond.

Alcohol has a real grip on this area – we could have ten teams here and it wouldn't be enough. In the period 2002–03 to 2009–10 the national figure for people with liver disease between 30–34 years of age rose by around 60 per cent. In our region overall it has risen by 403 per cent. If you look at our records for 2011, they show that we engaged with about 6,500 people, either in conversation or with practical help; we have assisted over 1,000 vulnerable adults, and defused eighty-six violent incidents. We have also directly prevented three people from committing suicide. Who knows what else we have prevented?

What I do know is that our volunteers approach their work with humility. They don't feel that they have much to bring to their role. They don't say, 'I can do this, I can do that', they just want to volunteer themselves. They volunteer in their weakness.

As a street pastor, and as co-ordinator for Newcastle Street Pastors, I start thinking about my Friday or Saturday night duty at the beginning of the week. I don't worry about it but I think about it in advance because it affects my diary . . . I don't want to put a lot in the diary for the weekend. After a night as a street pastor I feel as if I am jet-lagged! My normal routine is to go to bed at 10.30 p.m. and get up at 6.30 a.m., but if I'm going out with the team on a Friday night I will stay up late on the Thursday and sleep later on the Friday morning. That helps to prepare me for the late night on the Friday. I always spend more time in prayer as I get ready for a duty evening, partly to enable me to prepare a time of reflection for the other streets pastors before we go out.

During the day on Friday I might do some work from home, but not too much. I'll eat in the early evening and have a sleep before I go out. When my alarm goes off I'll have a shower to wake me up, then put the Street Pastors uniform on. I tend to wear ski pants or waterproof trousers as well as the rest of the gear. I always get to the base before the rest of the team and on my way there I usually stop to buy milk and biscuits. Some of the older ladies do a lot of baking and so we are well provided for. Once I have opened up the base and got all the kit together, I get the radios charged. Everyone else arrives at about 9.30 p.m.

We tend to spend about an hour with each other in fellowship, before starting the patrol at about 10.30 p.m. I lead us in a reflection and we pray together. It's beautiful to see the different ways that people pray. We are all from different churches, and we encourage everyone to pray the way they want to pray.

I'll be home again by about 5 a.m., though I don't go straight to bed. I tend to stay up and do some Facebook and Twitter for the Street Pastors team. We've got 400 followers on Facebook. Some of them will be awake through the night or have stayed up especially, so there are a small group of followers who respond to my tweets during the night. If my team is dealing with someone and I've got time, I tweet, but I don't give any details. Of course, we're always in touch with the group of prayer pastors back at base. Apart from specific situations that we can be involved in, or obvious needs, we have learned to 'feel' the atmosphere changing, and this is something that I always try to report back to people who are praying for us. Our local police have a word for this atmosphere; they say it's getting 'prickly'. They mean that something is about to go off.

One of the most difficult situations I've been in as a street pastor was the time I had a knife pulled on me. It happened when a girl asked me to pray for her. As I did so, she pulled a knife out and held it up to my face. Adrenalin kicked in, I stepped away and shouted, 'Get back' to the other street pastors who were nearby. I think I said to the girl, 'Don't come any closer.' After a few seconds one of her friends managed to pull her away. As I was getting my radio out to call the police I saw the girl hide the knife in a bush. British Transport police were in the vicinity, and they stopped the group of girls to take alcohol off them. Although we kept at a safe distance, we managed to get up to the officers and tell them that one of those girls had got a knife. Straight away the officers searched for the knife and found it in the bush. They wrapped the knife up, arrested the girl and put her in their van. We walked to the police station, along with one of the officers who was carrying the knife in a special bag.

On the way another fight kicked off, and the police officer gave me the bag with the knife in it to hold while he dealt with that situation. I didn't go back on patrol because I had to be interviewed by police. By the time the statement was done it was the end of our shift.

The next time I went out it was important for me to walk past the place where the incident happened to get rid of any fear. My wife is quite a calm character, she trusts in the Lord. She was concerned for my safety but she never once suggested that I should stop. She's totally on the same page as me. Her reaction was to pray for the person who pulled the knife. I later found out that the girl with the knife had, in the past, been visited by one of our street pastors and there was a reasonable relationship there. On the night of the incident the girl was just high, and all over the place. Her boyfriend had just been locked up and she was carrying the knife for protection.

I can't pretend that something like this doesn't have an effect on the team. Some street pastors left because of it. I hope you don't think I'm full of bravado; I have to consider the safety of other people as well as my own. Yet I didn't want to be defeated by my own fear. I feel God's work and his call is more important than my personal safety. The only thing that would stop me going back out is fear and God says 'Do not fear' (Isaiah 41:10).

My life changed drastically when I got involved with Street Pastors. At the age of twenty-five I was a regional account manager in the north of England, Scotland and Northern Ireland for a FTSE-100 software company. I hadn't done well at school but had worked my way up in the company to get this job, with a good salary, an Audi A4 and all the trappings that come with it. Around this time I became a Christian and that changed my perspective on everything. Up to this point my life had been driven by work, for the status and the money, which enabled me to buy a house and all the nice things I wanted.

About a year and a half after I became a Christian I went to a conference where I heard Tony Campolo speaking. Along with everyone else, I was passionately worshipping God. But to my surprise, Tony Campolo intervened in the worship and basically said, 'You guys are putting your hands in the air, worshipping a God who is passionate about the poor. How can you do that while you ignore the poor?' His aim was to encourage us to share our lives with the marginalised. It really impacted me and the people I was with.

With a group of friends I was part of a cell group, and out of that group, two or three of us had heard Tony Campolo speak at that conference. On a night out together, we were moving from one bar to another when a guy on the street stopped me and asked if I had any money. My immediate thought was, you're either going to drink it, smoke it or inject it (though I didn't say that out loud), so I hesitated. Tony Campolo's words came back to me and I responded by saying that I would buy the guy something to eat. That was the end of the night out for me. I took him to a kebab shop, sat down and had some food with him for about an hour.

The man started to speak about his life; how his girlfriend had left him and his family had disowned him because of his addiction to heroin. It dawned on me that he could have been one of my friends. He could have been me. He wasn't a bum . . . he had just fallen on hard times. I started weeping. He asked me why I was crying. I was hit by a strange sense of amazement that my life was any different to his. What was the reason that I was going home to a bed tonight while he was on the street? How had it happened that after all the drinking and partying I had done, I had somehow avoided the path that this man was now on? As the stranger watched me, all I could do in response was to pray. I prayed, God, whatever you want me to do to reach people like this man, I'll do it.

Me and the lads in the cell group started to look around to see what was going on in our area – which projects we could be part of that matched the response we wanted to make. We found nothing that we really wanted to be involved in, so we took the initiative and filled up a flask, made some sandwiches, prayed, and set off for an evening on the streets of Newcastle. My expectation was that the Lord would give us the name of a person or a street. What actually happened was that, as I prayed, I saw a feather in my mind's eye. I was a bit disappointed.

Undeterred, we went into the city centre on that Wednesday night and walked around for several hours without finding anyone at all that we could talk to or help. We were just about to go home when we noticed some movement behind a large waste bin around the back of the cathedral. A girl was crouching down in the small space behind the bin. We approached and reassured her we weren't going to hurt her. She told us about her life and that several years earlier she had been kidnapped and held hostage. She had not been able to return to normal life after this trauma. Her marriage had broken down and she had ended up on the streets. I said, 'Can we pray for you?' She said that was OK, so we started praying. As we prayed she looked up in the sky and started making noises. I stopped and asked if she was all right. She said, 'I can feel feathers falling on me.'

Feeling God's presence like that blew me away. By the time we left her, I knew that God was already out there on the streets of my city. I just needed to get out there and join him.

From this encounter with God and with the girl behind the waste bin, I knew what I needed to do. A few weeks later I was in the audience at another Christian conference where I heard Mike Royal talking about the work of Street Pastors in Birmingham. Once more, I was keenly aware of my own background and my thoughts moved to how my old life had centred around alcohol and drugs. I knew that Street Pastors fitted so well with me. I felt I could make a difference in the pub and club context.

I came home from that event with the desire to get Street Pastors started in Newcastle. I discovered that the dean of the cathedral was already thinking about a range of schemes, and Street Pastors was one of them. I said to myself that if the Street Pastors initiative gets off the ground and there's a job attached to it, wherever I am in my career, I am going to apply for it. When it was advertised, the job of coordinator for Newcastle Street Pastors was only three days a week, paying about £12,000. At that time I was earning between £30,000 and £40,000, plus the car. Seven people applied for the post. The interviewing panel were gracious to me. They said that I would be good at the job, but they were concerned about how I would cope with the reduction in my income. They were right to be concerned. It was not what I was used to.

Then, almost before I had had time to think this through, the global economic crisis hit home with startling results for me. I was told that my job in the software company was being given to someone coming back from maternity leave. My full-time post was going to become part-time, two days a week. I was offered a pro rata pay rise and the option of keeping the car. Basically I would be on a long-term secondment. With this arrangement in place, I accepted the Street Pastors job.

All this shows the way in which God answered my prayers about responding to people like the man I took to the kebab shop. God truly took me from one place and moved me, gradually, into another. But after six months of keeping both part-time jobs going, I was finding it difficult to balance the two. I felt God tell me to lay down the job at the software company. 'Am I hearing this right?' I asked. I was bewildered about my feelings and what I sensed God was saying to me. How many times had I acknowledged that God had set every-thing up so perfectly for me? These thoughts escalated while I was at a Christian conference in the United States and on the plane back home I took the decision to hand in my notice at the software company. As I walked into my house, the first thing I saw was a letter from the HR department offering me a voluntary redundancy package.

Of course my salary decreased again, but it was part of a step of faith for me. Newcastle Street Pastors was given £10,000 to pay my salary and run the whole project. It was all completely new ground for me. I think, typically, we often say to God, 'Yes, I'm ready, I'm on the diving board. Now fill the pool and I'll jump.' God's way is that we jump first, and he fills the pool later.

FAQ

What are the rights and wrongs of praying with a person who has had too much to drink?

I was always taught you can't evangelise a person who is drunk, but it's my experience that God's spirit is more powerful than anything that comes out of a bottle. In my area we've seen amazing spiritual realignment in people – very different outcomes from those I expected. The Street Pastors statement of purpose tells us that our role is primarily one of social action not spiritual progress, but sometimes the balance between these two changes.

Adrian, Street Pastors team coordinator

2

The night I met a street pastor: James

James doesn't remember much about the night he met Street Pastors Lynda and Becky, but the meeting was the beginning of the dramatic turnaround he needed.

A sex worker asked street pastors to get help for James, an alcoholic, who was squatting in a café where he used to work.

Lynda, a street pastor, remembers first seeing James sitting in a pool of urine with his legs splayed out, his head hanging down, arms between his legs.

'He looked so hopeless and dejected,' she says. 'His speech was slurred. He said to me, "I'm full of shit, I'm full of shit." We cleared up the place and helped him to his feet. "We're going to take you home," I told him, "so you can sleep."'

James, now a restaurant manager, can hardly remember that night, or the days that preceded it. 'I was having blackouts,' he says. 'I was used to working out what had happened to me from the physical evidence lying around when I woke up. One day I found myself lying on the floor in the hallway of my house next to a card that had come through the letterbox. There were two names on the card, Becky and Lynda, a phone number, and the words "Street Pastors". I felt near to death. I phoned Becky and Lynda. They came to my house. I said "I don't know who you are," and they sat in my front room while I threw up in the bathroom.

'I've always worked in the hospitality or retail sector. I love the job because I'm passionate about food and people. People like to gather in places like this and I get to meet loads of different characters from all over the world. I guess you would say that I'm curious about people. I'm sure it's a habit that started when I was a child, although I wasn't always sure what the correct behaviour with people was. I think I often acted inappropriately or got things wrong. Despite this my fascination with other people has stayed strong. I'm a people watcher because I'm always trying to fill in the blanks; I guess it's a lifetime project.

'It has not always been as harmless as it sounds. As a kid I had quite a few friends, though I wasn't close to any of them, and I brought people into my world to see what I could get out of the relationship. By the time I was a young adult I had a pretty warped idea about how relationships were conducted. My sense of alienation had increased and I was pretty materialistic. I lived within myself, in an unhealthy, isolated way. The personality I projected was a fabrication – there was hardly any of the real me in it. It didn't lead me anywhere good. I know that I've inflicted a lot of emotional damage on people around me.

'I've lived in the UK for thirteen years now, but I grew up in South Africa. My folks were from a poor, rural background but they had done well for themselves. I remember a fairly happy childhood. My dad was always working and studying at night. We were probably a typical family, but I remember feeling uneasy. I felt ill at ease around others, as if I was not sure what they wanted. It was a strange thing that became more accentuated as I grew up. When I was young I was molested and that had a dramatic influence on me. I'm not trying to blame everything that has happened on this incident, but there is a lot in my character that probably stems from it. It increased my feelings of alienation, I had problems trusting people, and my attitude was usually cynical. I would look at someone and think, "What's your angle?" I became someone who wanted to know what I was getting out of something. I was computing the world around me in those terms.

'My folks were religious people, and they raised me and my two sisters in the same way. We were forced to go to church, and the message from my parents was, "You will be confirmed but after that you can do what you want." I suppose that is what happened in the end – none of us children wanted to practise a faith. Later I became aware of a loss of faith in humanity as well as in God. People get deformed through life, and subconsciously you develop routines of thinking and codes of behaviour, but then there comes a time when you suddenly look at your life and there you are . . . all you can be really sure of is a deep sense of abandonment. One of my sisters died young, while she was training to be a vet, and when that happened I wondered where God was. I thought, why has God allowed this? I felt as if random events were God's personal vendetta.

'In my teens I was manipulative, calculating, sociopathic. I had no concern or empathy for others or any conception of how I hurt other people. I can't be sure whether I really, deliberately, recognised this at the time, but I think I took pleasure in the way that I behaved. Secretly I found it amusing, and feelings of compassion or regret rarely worried me. I had no ability to make proper connections between myself and other people. That's a fair appraisal. You have to say that what a person amounts to is a summary of their actions: you may have a tsunami of emotions going on inside, but actions are what people judge you by.

'My first job in my mid-teens was selling drugs, doing pick-ups and drop-offs for the dealers. I was also a foot soldier working for gangs involved in low-level organised crime. I'm a big guy, and that always counted in my favour; plus, I wasn't shy to put myself forward for jobs. I had an aptitude for the life of crime: I was charismatic and intelligent, and those things were useful. I was not just somebody who went around whacking people. I was a persuasive person, with an ability to bring people around. I could read people really well and was a bit of a chameleon, with a pretty good line in emotional blackmail. Back then my people-watching habit involved storing up pieces of information about my friends so that, at some point, I could apply that knowledge to my advantage. I created mental maps about people made up of little details anyone else would think were irrelevant. But I was playing the long game. I think I probably lost all grip on reality. I thought I was in control, but ultimately I was eaten up by that control – the very thing I was seeking.

'I took to drugs and alcohol like a fish to water. Alcohol and cannabis were prolific in the small town where I lived so it was just a question of what I could lay my hands on. Alcohol pervaded everything I did. At first it was the only thing that was available to me but later everything else became available too. I've never understood why alcohol is separated out from the drug family – it's still a path to oblivion and a means to an end like all the other substances. Many of the drugs sharpened the feelings I had about myself and other people. I have no doubt that I was born an addict, with addictive patterns of thought. I recognised addiction in myself. I knew its name. It was like watching an old acquaintance walk towards me.

'I slipped from one job to another. I needed work as it was a useful cover for the money I earned from dealing. If a boss gave me any lip, I would tell them where to stick their job. I got fired from a lot of jobs. This way of life continued into my twenties.

'I was repeatedly diagnosed with bipolar depression. Now, in my forties, my understanding of the illness and the correct medication eases me tremendously. I have some relief from it now, because I am ready to be helped. But at sixteen, when I was first told I was manically depressed, I laughed. With a grin on my face I said, "Do I look depressed?" I thought depression was someone snivelling in the corner. I didn't know it could be someone bursting with energy, almost tripping over their thoughts and feelings.

'By this time I had moved from the backwater where my family lived to Cape Town, but my options were running out as far as work was concerned. I wanted to leave South Africa, but with a South African passport you can only stay in another country for two years. My cousins had done that – come to the UK for two years and then gone home again – but that wasn't good enough for me. I resolved that I would have proper access to a life in the UK from the start. I needed to extricate myself from the drug scene. Seeing friends in the same line of work getting murdered was not something I was keen on. When I was 24, I married a girl called Madeleine. She was clever, good looking and a foreign national. Three years later, within a year of receiving a Belgian passport and moving to England, we were divorced. It was not a coincidence. I pulled a lot of pieces out of her. I was such a good liar that I even believed myself.

'Things were going wrong. I might have been in a new country but I had travelled with baggage. I lived first in London, trying to keep a low profile, but I was so dominated by my thought patterns that I didn't stand a chance of doing anything else. My anxiety reached almost unbearable levels. My sister died, and I didn't even know how to think about that, how to process it. My addictions escalated. Despite all the evidence, I always thought that a proper life, that I was in control of, was within reach.

'I can't clearly remember large portions of those years. I ended up in hospital, connected to more tubes than I could count. My body had wasted away, and eventually I learned that I had been in a coma for three months after developing pancreatitis, followed by septicaemia, and my lungs had collapsed. I was amazed to find that my dad had flown over and been with me for a month and gone back home without me ever waking up. For much of this time it was thought I wouldn't live, but I eventually left hospital after six months.

'This happened in 2003. When I left hospital I was pretty much a broken man. I had to learn to walk and talk again. I had nowhere to live, but there were one or two good people that I managed to stay with on and off. Madeleine wanted nothing to do with me, understandably. I spent most of that year in a daze, full of fear and pain, in turmoil. I was weak for the first time in my life. I don't want to be over-dramatic about this, but I had an unbelievable sense of survivor's guilt. I really shouldn't have been alive. This kicked off another downward spiral of depression. I spent a massive amount of time walking around, almost manically, with the same thoughts running around my head: why did my sister die? Why did some of my friends die? Why am I still here, when I've been so wicked?

'Physically I was slowly regaining my strength, although all my stomach muscles were ruptured because I had been operated on so many times. This led to a stomach hernia, for which I had to go back into hospital for another operation. I was desperately frightened at being so weak. I started to get back to what was 'normal' for me: chiefly, drinking and dating. It was a futile effort to get my life back on track, but it was founded on all kinds of untruths and lies. Anyway, I had just enough cockiness to meet and begin to date Genevieve. I knew that she was going to be the mother of my children from the moment I met her. All the girls I had known before lived in the same world as me, and therefore I had never entertained the idea of children before, as it was obvious to me that they would not have been suitable mothers. I guess I didn't have as many scruples about fatherhood.

'I was fascinated by Genevieve. She was a Christian and she'd never done any drugs. I'd never met a creature like that! We were married six months after we met and Genevieve was pregnant with our son one week later. On the recommendation of my bank manager, we began to look for a house to buy in Leighton Buzzard, where houses were more affordable. I was desperate to get the hang of an 'honest' life. There were a few glimpses of it – the wife, the bank manager, the house – but they didn't make a complete picture. The codes of behaviour, the ethics that I needed for an 'honest' life were incomprehensible to me. None of that stuff about getting to your job at the right time, doing the job all day as instructed, bringing home wages, spending them sensibly, none of it made any sense to me. I didn't know how to function in that life. It was really difficult for me and I went through a succession of jobs. Genevieve genuinely loved me, she wanted to try to help. We even had another child, because I pulled what was left of my life together and convinced her that it was a good idea. Yet by the time our second child was born, our marriage was finished. When I was arrested and had to face the real possibility of going to prison, Genevieve immediately started divorce proceedings. After the hearings it was concluded that there wasn't enough evidence to convict me and I escaped prison.

'Though I found it impossible to work for anyone else, I found I could work a little more successfully for myself. For a time I had two businesses, but in time I managed to screw them up because I couldn't commit to anything properly. As the businesses slipped through my fingers, I built up a mountain of debt and filed for bankruptcy, owing about £15,000. The fragile walls of my life caved in on me again, and I was in and out of hospital. My body didn't want to function any more. I was operated on twice, the second one nearly killing me. I was told I couldn't drink any more. I felt utterly forsaken. That was about six months ago.

'After my businesses collapsed I took a job in a café and started to try to face the consequences of what I had been

doing with my life. It was too big a task. There was one occasion, not long before I met the street pastors, that I turned up
drunk at the family home where Genevieve and the children
lived. I had always tried to shield the children from my drinking
and I was plunged into desperation when I realised that I had
staggered down the path to the front door with a bottle of
vodka in my hand. It was a new level of depravity. I thought I
was truly capable of anything now.

'For the next two weeks I was permanently drunk. I had the
keys to the café where I worked and I just kept going back
there, day or night, sometimes thinking I could do a shift, even
trying to cook, mainly just crashing out. Nobody could get me
out of there. In the end they had to shut the café. It was while
I was trying to get the keys in the lock of the café door one
night that I was seen by a local lady who went to get help from
street pastors.'

Lynda was one of the street pastors who found James that
night. She recalls: 'It was not long after 10 p.m. The four of us
had checked in with the door staff at a variety of clubs, had a
chat with them and made sure they knew which of us was out
that night. We were heading towards Tesco, our usual stop for
a toilet break. It was early and still quiet. We heard a voice
calling to us and realised that coming up behind us was a local
lady, a sex worker, who we regularly said "Hi" to. We often saw
her out at night, but this time it was more than a greeting she
wanted to pass on. "You guys need to go to the café," she told
us, "James is in trouble. Can you help him get home safely?"
She told us how she had found James on the doorstep of the
café, trying to let himself in. She had taken the keys from him,
opened the door, pushed him inside and then put the keys
through the letterbox. She had felt he would be safer in there
than outside. Her next thought had been to come and find us.

'We were only a quarter of a mile from the café and we headed
there straight away. We could see James inside, sitting in a pool

of urine. We called through the letterbox and asked him to put the keys back through to us so that we could come in. He managed to do this and two of us stayed outside the building while two went inside, one man and one woman. After about ten minutes the two of us who were outside opened the door and joined the others. James was now sitting on a sofa in the window. He looked up and said to me, "I'm full of shit, I'm full of shit." Everyone else said politely, "No, you're not, no, you're not," but I said, "You're right, you are. But you won't be like this forever."

'I was the right person in the right place, because I knew how he felt. As he stared at the floor I told him I was an American and I knew how it felt to move to a country where people spoke the same language but meant different things. I knew what it was like to belong but feel outside. I was also a recovering alcoholic, with twenty-one sober years behind me. "Right now," I said to James, "we can sit and talk and one of three things will probably happen. You will cry, you will fight, you will pass out. So get up, we're going to take you home so you can sleep."

'While we were there the phone rang. It was his ex-wife, she was yelling at him and he was yelling back. He wanted to see his kids the next day. After the phone call he was even more dejected. We used that to motivate him to get home. "You need to get home, change your clothes, and get ready to see your kids," we said. One of the other street pastors mopped up the floor so that we could leave the café ready for business the next day.

'We got the address out of him and made him walk, with one arm around Becky and one arm around me. He wasn't happy about walking and muttered "You bastards" virtually all the way. He is a big man and we weaved from side to side, but I knew that as long as we could keep him moving we would get there. At his front door, he produced a key and we opened the door. He didn't want to lie down. The room we went into was dark and cluttered. He seemed ready to be left.

'The next morning, Sunday, Becky dropped a card through James's letterbox, with a note on it telling him he could call Street Pastors any time. I think it also said that if he wanted us to, we would call round to the house to talk.'

James continues the story. 'I'm not sure what happened to me the next day, but I noticed some time later that my wrists were bruised and marked from handcuffs. I must have carried on drinking and been arrested and then taken to hospital. Monday arrived. I was aware that the mobile health team were going to come out and see me. I called those street pastors and they came round to my house on the same morning. One of them, called Lynda, told me that AA had saved her life. I replied, "I couldn't do that, I'll do it on my own. I'll do it with my will-power." I remember Lynda leaning towards me and saying, quite gently, "How is that working for you, James?" That really pierced me. She didn't want to argue with me, she just wanted me to ask the question of myself. Lynda said she would find out when the next AA meeting was. Then they took me out for breakfast in town.

'The next AA meeting turned out to be the following day and, true to their word, Lynda and Becky came back and took me to the group. It was a "Step 3" meeting and Step 3 is entitled, "Make a decision to turn our will and our lives over to the care of God as we understand Him." The room was full of people wrestling with the things I wrestle with and saying how difficult it had been for them, how it had taken them two years or more, but they had kept trying and kept coming to meetings.

'Lynda and Becky sat through it with me. For the first two months I was numb, but I kept going to meetings and listened to everything that was said. A few months further down the line, I have good days and bad days. On the bad days, when I make the wrong decision, get sloppy or lazy and don't work my

AA programme enough, I write 'TWBD' between the tattoos on my arm: Thy will be done. I live by little increments, just like they say at AA, one step at a time. I have learned to deal with life in the exact moment I am in. As soon as I think about anything more, my mind just revolts. It is life in bite-sizes, I suppose, but it actually reminds me that God has been with me in thousands of instances, in all the pieces of my life. Lynda and Becky say that I have a big heart. I want to help everyone else I come across so I often fill my car up with other people and we go to AA – together.'

PART TWO

Les's Faith Journey Begins

@angelatrew18h
3 Story Evangelism at #SH2013. Faith sharing, should we? How?
@StreetPastors one good way. Loving, caring, practical help.

3

1963–1990:
My search

My curiosity about the Christian faith was woken one day by a chance encounter with an elderly Nigerian man named Amos, who offered me a cup of tea while I was out shopping for a machete. Conflict with my father had escalated and after our fight the day before I wanted to show him I was no longer a kid he could order around.

Frustrated, I resolved that the only thing to do was to go out and get a machete. My anger ran high for several hours and, even when I woke the following day, the purchase of the weapon was still uppermost in my mind. With the smooth leather of its handle in my grip, I would bring my father to submission. It was a Monday morning and I went to work as usual, planning to make my purchase at lunch time. As my lunch break approached, I was told they couldn't do without me in the kitchen, so I had several more hours to pass before I could call in at the army surplus store on my way home.

My route to the store went past the restaurant where my cousin George worked as a chef. I thought it was a good opportunity to catch up with him, as it was only minutes until he clocked off. I looked around for somewhere to wait. Adjoining the restaurant was a mission hall, with an open door leading onto the street. I poked my head around the door and met the

41

glance of a skinny black man sitting in the corner, sipping a cup of tea.

He introduced himself as Amos, and told me he was a preacher. It quickly became clear to me that talking was Amos's favourite pastime. Despite my plan to have a chat with George and the burning pressure to get my hands on a machete, I stepped inside, accepted a cup of tea and made some polite replies to Amos's questions.

I was eagerly devouring the teachings of Ras Tafari at the time and was quick to engage with preaching or philosophical discussion of any kind whenever I could. Rastafarianism had caught my mind and my imagination and I loved the feeling that I was searching and finding all in one deep step of faith. I guess it was this same interest in spirituality that helped me to recognise a purposefulness and energy in Amos, small and slight as he was. As he invited me to sit with him and started to speak, I realised that he was a Christian and, more than that, he was the type of Christian who did not believe in luck or chance. So when he saw me that day, an angry youth, Amos was ready to preach. He spoke with passion, with one hand tightly gripping his tea cup and the other arm variously waving, pointing and slapping the table. The way he told me the story of Jesus made it almost appear on a screen before my eyes. I could see Calvary, I could see the soldiers, I could hear the thud of hammer on nail and the cry of agony as the huge wooden cross thudded home into the slot and Jesus was left to die.

This mission hall is where my journey into the Christian faith began. I started to talk with God. The vivid description Amos had given me had created an atmosphere in which I just seemed to be able to commune with the One, for whom – through Rastafarianism, the haze of ganja and the fight for hope and survival – I had been searching. And, after all my efforts, it was God who spoke first.

'Les, Rasta is not the way,' the voice in my mind said.

'Selassie is not the way. I am the way. And I am the truth and the life as well. Les, depart from your sin.'

I said goodbye to Amos and promised to come back to talk some more. During the half-hour walk home, I knew I had been talking to Someone as clearly as if it had been a conversation with my brother. And as I walked, I decided I wanted to become a Christian. I wanted to know God. At that moment an awe-inspiring fear came upon me, a fear of judgement, a fear that if I were to die or this Jesus Amos had told me about were to come back there and then, I would have no excuses and I would be lost. And what could I say to the Son of God? I then had one of those experiences normally reserved for people facing death, when I saw in an instant my whole life spread before me. It didn't look good.

My parents had come to London from Antigua at the beginning of the 1960s, in the days when Enoch Powell toured the Caribbean looking for workers who would rally round the war-torn motherland. There were jobs available that English men and women didn't want to do – driving buses and trains or working on the factory production line. Mum and Dad never intended to settle in London. They planned to work for a couple of years and then return to their children, the four of us, who were cared for by my grandmother in the two years that they were away. Things didn't go to plan for them, and so they decided that, rather than be away from their children for any longer, they would arrange for us to make the same journey and join them in London.

In the days when 'Rule Britannia' was sung with fervour, working people like my parents heard the British government's call for help and responded, both in their own interest and those of the Commonwealth. They saw the motherland as a place of opportunity for their children. Our children have got a chance here, they believed. Education is free. Our standard of living will be higher.

Yet it was a difficult time for my parents. My father had to work hard, and once us children had arrived, my mother couldn't work because she was looking after us. We lived in a damp basement flat. Getting anything better than this was extremely difficult. The private rental market was challenging for a family like mine. Anywhere decent was very expensive. Even places that were less than decent might display a sign in the window that read, 'No Irish, no blacks, no dogs'. The poor conditions of the cramped flat in Islington had a damaging effect on my mother's health. My parents were very determined people, but the cracks that were already opening up in their relationship back home were made far worse by the pressures they were under in London. Some West Indian couples found that they pulled together and were stronger in these circumstances. Others struggled as existing problems were compounded by the strains. My parents separated when I was seven, two years after I had arrived in Britain.

Although Dad moved to a room that was only four streets away from the rest of the family, not having him around made me feel insecure. I remember acutely the profound effects of my parents' separation. As a child, particularly a child in a West Indian home, I wasn't encouraged to articulate my feelings, my sorrow or my pain. Children were seen and not heard, and I had no voice or opinion that would be listened to. I remember thinking that I would make sure my own children never had to experience this.

My mother was pregnant at the time that my father left and so it was not until this youngest child reached nursery school age that she was able to find work to support herself and us. Naturally her return to work had implications for the rest of the family. She was away for long periods of time, leaving us in the care of my older sisters in the morning, returning at some point in the day to prepare a meal for us, and then going back to work, not coming home until the middle of the evening.

I had questions that nobody seemed to want to answer. White people hated me, therefore I questioned my identity. I asked myself, what is a West Indian? What is important about my African roots? The Atlantic triangle and slavery were big issues that I was aware of but had no answers for. At home, at school and at church, nobody spoke about these things. Through the news and images of race relations in America, I got to know some of the high-profile names, faces and politics that I knew were somehow relevant to the circumstances of my own life. Through the legacy of Malcolm X and the activities of Angela Davis and the Black Panther Party in the civil rights movement, I got a glimpse of the kind of questions that could be asked and the kind of answers that might be given.

During the last two years of primary school, I began to express my confusion and my questions in a physical way. I had some great teachers but there were others that were prejudiced. I became aware that I was pigeonholed; I was simply a black kid. It wasn't a level playing field. I felt powerless because I had been brought here as a result of my parents' decision and I couldn't see any way of returning to Antigua. This was a time of tension between young black youths and the police, and besides this there was tension between the way children were brought up in a British family and the way they were brought up in a West Indian family. Many black teenagers were taken into care as a result of this cultural conflict. As children we were brought up to respect our elders with a high importance placed on manners. A smack or chastisement was quite normal at home in the Caribbean (I once had to have three stitches in my head after my mother hit me), but in Britain reports were made to social services and before you knew it a child was gone, taken into care. My mother's sudden outbursts were, no doubt, caused by the pressure she was under. She had money worries, she was lonely, and she was living under the same discrimination as me. People do harsh things under that kind of pressure.

In my first primary school I was ostracised by a group of white kids. By the time I had been transferred to another primary school, I determined that no one was going to take advantage of me. I became hard, aggressive. It was just me thinking that I'd had enough. I'm not saying it was right. It turned me into an ugly person.

When I was ten my family moved to a large housing estate in Camden. We were the first black family to move in. We were conspicuous, but my brother Vernon and I refused to be bullied, making as many friends as we could among the white kids in the neighbourhood. It was a peace that was regularly interrupted by the arrival of older boys who passed through the area shouting their taunts of 'nigger' and 'wog'. At secondary school I discovered my temper and my strength and gained a reputation as one of the best fighters in the school. With a small group of my close friends, I learned to leave school for long periods during the day, finding a back way into the cinema, raiding the cash boxes in phone booths and seeing the school day out playing pinball or table football. I grew accustomed to walking around with my right hand permanently in my jacket pocket, feeling the reassurance of the cold blade of my flick knife. My friends and I wore skinhead gear. I liked to be smartly dressed in my Sta Prest mod trousers or turned-up Levi jeans and my heavy Doc Marten boots.

Local skirmishes between rival groups of skinheads were another focus for my attention. Trouble could begin to brew over the smallest aggravation and then word would go around that the Finchley skinheads were looking for revenge or the Archway skinheads were openly challenging for a brawl. I was involved in some large-scale crew fights around north London, many that brought fear and devastation to residents, shops and businesses. We would be armed with bicycle chains and axe handles, and even when the police had arrived and we had made a run for our escape routes, the rush of adrenalin often meant that we'd look for an opportunity for theft or intimidation on our way home. I was battle-hardened at the age of thirteen.

Such fights often left me feeling empty and fixated on the next time that a clash would break out, when I hoped for more recruits and better weapons. The aggression was one way to express my awareness of what was happening around me, and what it meant for me. My anger and confusion and the music that I was into told me that I needed to put up a fight. Bob Marley's 'Get Up, Stand Up' fired my resolve to say 'Enough is enough'. I wondered why my parents had brought me to a land where I would have to struggle to make a go of life. More and more, my young life revolved around aggressive resistance to what I was experiencing at home, at school, on the streets . . . even on a simple trip down the road to buy groceries. I was ruled by my emotions, in survival mode.

On the day that I planned to buy a machete, I had argued with my father. Fists had been clenched, though not used, but violence between the two of us was often simmering under the surface. Dad had come back to live with us children after the death of my mother in 1974. Our sense of loss and bewilderment was aggravated by my father's decision to move in with us. There was no discussion or consultation about this, and reintegrating a father into a household of young adults was a tense and difficult process. One minute he wasn't there, the next minute he was. That was the start of real problems between us.

My dad lacked diplomacy, he didn't communicate. He was an old-school Caribbean father: whatever he said was right. He obviously felt hurt about things that had happened in our family and in his marriage, but he never let go of those things. To his credit he hadn't walked away when his marriage broke down, he still spent time with us, but over time he became more distant and struggled to come to terms with the fact that we were growing up. My views, and the fact that I wanted to express them, were a problem. I tried not to be disrespectful but I didn't want to shy away from speaking my mind. He, on the other hand, found it insulting that his boy was expressing an opinion.

The main bone of contention was the way that I would stay away from home for days at a time without announcing my plans.

'Where you sleep, boy?' he would ask. 'Listen me, boy. No more dem sleepin' out.'

And my reply would come, tense and angry, 'Watcha, Dad, you no talkin' to a boy, you are dealin' with a man.'

'If you think you more man than me, sleep out again an' see what happens.'

Around about the age of sixteen, the music and clothes and parties of Rastamen began to get a hold on me. I spent whole nights at 'Blues', West Indian parties where you paid an entrance fee on the door of an ordinary terraced house and then spent the night enjoying the loud music and the beer. I liked to buy my fifty-pence worth of ganja, neatly folded in a piece of newspaper, and roll a spliff for a pleasant evening's smoke. There was a marked contrast between this way of living and the violence of the crew fights. I found I was tired of fighting and ready for the spiritual and physical sensation of being at peace with my surroundings and the joy of fellowship with other West Indians.

Yet, even through the haze of ganja smoke, I knew there was anger among my brothers. The questions about identity and oppression that had been turning over in my mind since childhood were calling me into this new faith, but behind the party spirit there was restlessness and even sadness. I hailed Ras Tafari (Emperor Haile Selassie) as my king and saviour. I sang about him, I read about him, I talked endlessly about him. Here was a way of fashioning my own identity in relation to a divine being and to Africa. As a Rasta I held the natural and the spiritual in tension – the desire for freedom from oppression ran parallel to the desire for forgiveness and peace. The spiritual element of Rastafarianism was found in meditation about Africa and the reappropriation of my African past, the rejection of slavery and the hope of a freedom that would release me from my natural situation. I was attracted by everything that I saw in Ras Tafari and my fellow Rastamen. Selassie, the mystical being, the new 'Jesus' for black men, would help me to get to Africa one day.

My new faith was a bitter disappointment to my family. We were brought up to dress smartly with a nice haircut and to have good manners so, culturally speaking, being a Rasta brought shame upon the family. There was fear that I would be seen by the police to be a drug dealer. As the family tearaway, the unpredictable one, my mother had prayed fervently for me at the Methodist chapel where she had worshipped. Here I was again, letting everyone down.

I spent about twelve months enquiring into Rastafarianism, taking its beliefs as my own and searching for a truth I could build my life upon. My faith in Selassie began to crumble the day I saw pictures of him on television. I had an immediate awakening that told me that this man was a mere mortal, just a well-dressed man climbing out of an expensive limousine in Addis Ababa. Though I was still trapped in the belief that I must search deeply into questions of faith with my Rasta brothers, I had acknowledged that Selassie, if he was anything, was a God for black people; he was no universal God. His death in 1974 only left me feeling even more disillusioned, questioning my worship of a dead hero.

On the day that I came across Amos, the preacher drinking his tea in the mission hall, I learned that knowing Jesus meant knowing that he had made it possible for me to have a relationship with God. Where I had believed that what was important was striving to do everything in my power to search for and establish a new identity for myself, God in Jesus had done that for me. He loved me so much that, despite my condition, he had sent his Son to earth to die for me. God was willing to accept and receive me just as I was.

When I arrived home after my talk with Amos – without a machete – I announced to my family that I was going to become a Christian. They ignored me and carried on watching television.

'I am goin' to become a Christian,' I repeated.

'Oh yeah?' said my sister, Lemina, without any interest whatsoever. 'You always comin' up with crazy ideas. Leave us alone cos we are watchin' dis programme.'

I went to my room, and there I stayed all night, although I was unable to sleep for thinking about God. I thought about the death of Jesus as described by Amos, and I thought about the possibility of Christ returning when I wasn't ready for it. I decided that after work the next day, I would go straight to Amos and talk some more with him.

But I couldn't find Amos that day after work, and I couldn't find the final piece of the jigsaw that I knew would give me peace of mind. I couldn't sleep for several nights. I became bleary-eyed and sluggish at work. I felt as though my life was full of poison that needed to be removed, but I didn't know how to go about it and I didn't know how to pray; I felt dumb. Instead tears came into my eyes. I felt guilty and so dirty before the Almighty God, whose presence I could feel. The stronger the presence of God became, the fouler and dirtier I felt.

I struggled to speak any words of prayer. I tried to say the Lord's Prayer, but as I opened my mouth to try to speak, sobs rose up from deep inside me. I could only say, 'Jesus, if you are real, I want you to save me.'

After what seemed like a long time I got off my knees, and stood in front of my full-length wardrobe mirror.

'Wotcha, a big man like you cryin'?' I said to the reflection. Time passed as I stood there, trying to reconcile the image of myself with the new spirit within me. Over the days that followed I threw out all the ganja that I possessed and had my locks cut off. I wanted people to know that I was a child of God, and I didn't need locks to do that.

I got back in contact with Amos and spent many hours with him, receiving his encouragement and teaching. He told me of a church in Vauxhall where he would take me and where I would feel at home. Every day I encountered the reactions of my family, old friends, other boys from the Archway gang, workmates. They were all watching me, shocked at my new appearance and waiting to see how a fiery teenager like me would get on as a Christian. My father, with whom I was still re-establishing a relationship, was very sceptical about my sudden desire to go to church. He didn't ask me anything about it directly, but got his information from my brothers and sisters. It was his belief that I was going to church to look for girls.

My general approach was to announce 'I've become a Christian' to whoever I met, and go on from there, often with so much fervour that I was oblivious to whether my audience was interested or not, or how much shock and disbelief was registering on their faces.

'I gave my life to Jesus,' I told one family friend, 'and between us we decided that the locks must go. I also threw my ganja away, 'cos I'm a new person.'

I took a strong stance against the things I had done in my former life, and immediately told my friends I wouldn't be joining them at the club or the rave, or sleeping around or accepting their offers of a spliff. I was quite clear about my new boundaries. I was quick to tell anyone and everyone that my life had been a mess, and that I needed to let God take over and help me get things straight. So I searched and I searched, I asked people, and eventually I found out that all you have to do is ask God's forgiveness, receive his love, and let him come right in. It's called being born again.

I was aware of a warm glow inside me as I formed the words and I realised that although I spoke with immaturity and a lack of tact, God had been speaking through me. The joy of speaking for the Lord who now meant so much to me gripped my imagination. It was not all plain sailing. At work my colleagues didn't want to know that Jesus loved them. They were threatened by what I said and reacted by ridiculing me. I was indignant and reverted to what I knew best, aggression, matching their taunts with threats. My dream of speaking gloriously about my faith was temporarily shattered. These early days in my Christian journey were characterised by such highs and lows.

But God showed me that his victory over death meant the height of rejection for Jesus. I saw that the response to scoffing and hostility was to love my enemies, following the example that Jesus gave. I came to understand better that the Christian life was not going to be a series of happy events, but it would be a battle between spiritual powers. As I read more of the Bible I discovered that it was by God's spirit, not by might or by power, that a person would come to see God for themselves. This was the way that God had patiently revealed himself in my own life and, in contrast, I realised that what I had been doing was forcing God onto people, probably doing more harm than good. As I came to understand this more I began to pray. 'Help me to speak to people. Help me to speak your words, and to speak them the way you want me to speak them. Help me to really love people.' And as I prayed I had a growing certainty that when I talked to people about Jesus, God would save them. I just knew that this was how it would be.

Some friendships disintegrated after I became a Christian, but others came in their place. Davison was one of them. We met at his church in Haringey, which was holding a convention on a Saturday night. I loved the idea of being in church on a Saturday night rather than in a club and, as we chatted enthusiastically, Davison introduced me to a friend of his, Mike. At the end of the evening the conversation continued in my battered Ford Cortina as I drove Mike and Davison home. As we slowed down in heavy traffic, we watched a long line of people queuing on the pavement to get into the cinema. Mike, who was a home-movie buff, twisted around in the front seat to speak excitedly.

'These people need Jesus,' he said, his face coming alive. 'Hey, why don't we buy a projector and find somewhere to show Christian films?' We nodded in agreement. The idea took hold of all of us. I knew straightaway that film was a good way to relate to young people and would help me get across the message I wanted to share. I listened as Mike and Davison talked about the need for prayer before we started this venture, and grew nervous as they went on to propose that we fasted for three days and three nights in preparation. I suddenly saw that there was going to be a personal cost if I was to be successful in evangelism.

We prayed at my sister Lemina's house, a venue that was offered to us because she was in need of a babysitter for her young children. Our aim was to prepare the way in prayer for the film-showing ministry and ask God to help us to be effective. Ahead of us lay uncertainties about where we would get the money to buy a projector and hire the films. But we meant business. We started to call our ministry a 'film roadshow', and bookings came in thick and fast as I contacted old friends in youth clubs around London. Davison's church took a special offering for our work and this enabled us to buy a projector. We found that many youth workers were keen to book us to show a film to their kids and that most people were far more enthusiastic about watching a film than about listening to a guest speaker. It was my job to 'sum up' after the film, and I found great liberty in doing this. We saw many people, young people, parents and kids, surrender their lives to God.

We took the films to churches and schools and I spoke to

audiences that were embarrassed, deeply thoughtful, inquisitive or menacing. Many times I found myself talking to groups in which Rastafarianism was rife. There was a common attitude that the Church had exploited black people, and anyone seen to be joining the 'white man's religion' was regarded with suspicion, sometimes hatred.

'I used to be a Rasta,' I would say, 'but it didn't make sense to me when Selassie died. Then I turned to Jesus, and he completely changed my life, because he's alive.' I emphasised the contrast between Jesus, risen from the dead, and Selassie, a dead man like any other. I would explain just how I got to the point where I discovered the truth and what it meant to me now. I found I had the same ability to connect with skinheads. I had the language, the cultural references, and I realised that it helped to make me a person that Rastas and skinheads could respect. I could speak their language, and when they spoke, they were speaking mine. Many kids couldn't speak the typical Christian 'language' that, all too often, many of us use without thinking. Of course I came across many people who were bitter and hardened, and those that were cynical about the Church, but I would tell them that though they may have been let down by the search for truth and peace, or by a church, or by the empty worship of 'inspiring' people or cults, God would never fail them.

I frequently found myself drawing on the trauma and the challenges of my life as it was before I became a Christian; it was a part of my life that was still quite vivid in my memory, and only really a few months in the past. The desire and the ability to show others that God had changed me was strong in those early days, and it has never left me. My background and my experience of life had been, at times, very traumatic and challenging, sometimes bordering on the catastrophic. I understood how it felt to be marginalised, to feel desperate and vulnerable. I recognised the hopelessness in the eyes of many young people. When I connected with other people, I had a sense of fearlessness as I spoke, and I talked to them of hope because I knew that human lives could be changed for the better.

Developing gifts

In 1980, as I turned twenty-three, my faith was growing in security and I had a pleasing sense that my life was important to God. I knew that God was working out his plans in me – there was purpose to my life! Around this time I first met Andrew Brandon, an evangelist like me. We met at a film-showing in a church in Kentish Town, after which Andrew, always well-spoken, addressed the audience. As we discussed the evening after everyone had gone home, Andrew suggested that we meet again, 'to see if we could do something together'. I was drawn to Andrew's evident care for people living in his community and his sacrificial attitude. In addition, I liked the idea of the black/white partnership that we would form and imagined that this would have a meaningful impact as we worked together in London's mixed-race neighbourhoods. We went on to become partners in missions, gospel concerts, film shows and rallies, often with a focus on locations where there was hate and unrest, demonstrating a no-holds-barred approach when we spoke to the young people who packed out the venues. I experienced the great thrill of bringing others into the kingdom with me and I learned to 'let go' with passion and spontaneity in my preaching during this time.

When I was growing up, Sunday was the worst day of the week. It would begin with my mother saying that she would 'baptise' me with a jug of cold water if she had to ask me one more time to get out of bed. When I had squeezed myself into my Sunday suit and tie, I would follow her to the church and begin the endurance test that was the Sunday service. Sitting next to my mum, on the hardest of hard pews, there was always a strong possibility that I would get her right hand of fellowship (a cuff round the ear) either to encourage me to sing up or remind me to be quiet. To overcome the boredom of listening to the preaching, I would check out the numbers of the hymns that were planned for the service to see which one had the most verses. I knew that it was not just me, but most children of my acquaintance, who would have no hesitation in declaring that the dullness of the preaching was at the top of the list of things that turned them off church. The memory of Sunday's boredom, and the fear of stepping out of line as a child in church, shaped the way I engaged with audiences as a communicator.

In the early 1980s, as I discovered that I was good at communicating truths about God, I began to have small opportunities to make sure that church was not a place where everything that happened was an academic exercise in learning or listening. Instinctively I knew that preaching must be about engaging with your audience, getting participation, being lively, dynamic and relevant and relying on the work of the Spirit to help others understand what I was saying. As a young man, the potential of my preaching gift was mentored and cultivated by mature church leaders. James Cain, the superintendent of several churches, and David Perry, the minister of the church in Vauxhall where I was baptised, along with Andrew Brandon, were mentors to me at this time. James and David saw potential in me and, to help me develop my preaching ministry, they made me part of the preaching plan, gave me feedback, allowed me to travel with them on pastoral visits and gave me responsibilities in the local congregation.

In 1981, newly married, I began to form plans to work full time as an evangelist. I was working as a training officer in a transport company and all my speaking engagements or film roadshow events were fitted into evenings and weekends and my boss, Tom, allowed me time off for the missions that Andrew Brandon and I led together. Over the years this developed into an arrangement which allowed me to take one week off work every month in order to fulfil my speaking commitments. So there was little surprise for Tom when I eventually handed in my resignation in October 1985. I enrolled at London Bible College, knowing that it was right at this important juncture in my life to put in place a theological foundation, and to spend time understanding the Bible and thinking through my beliefs. It was an important time of preparation, but I questioned how effective the training was at making me a relevant leader. More than half of the things I did then as an evangelist and church leader I did without any specific formal training. This reinforced to me the need to spend time alongside other leaders (in the Church and outside it) who were working in the community; to immerse myself in a totally non-Christian environment and get involved in the issues that coloured the neighbourhood in which I lived, whether that might be mental health care, political agendas, or cultural affiliations. I found I needed to eat with people, socialise with people, and see the community through their eyes.

Whatever race or ethnic background a person belongs to, we must remember our common humanity. We all have feelings, senses and emotional pains. Those things come first. I have always tried to relate to the big issues of a person's life, always with humility. People very quickly pick up on our motives for helping them. If our motives are good they will respond and they will understand that our motive is to help them. You don't have to have lived the same life as the people you are trying to communicate with. I've seen sharp-suited lawyers and bankers leave their jobs in the City at lunch time to join me in outreach events and they have not been limited in their capacity to relate to young people from council estates. Speaking the right 'language' is important in some ways and unimportant in other ways. Respect and a generous heart are more important. Time has a premium and people know when someone is willing to share their premium with them.

In the first years of my Christian ministry, I explored the boundaries of cross-cultural communication that often influence our contact with other people. It was a time when I had the opportunity to meet a very wide group of people inside and outside of the Church. I learned that my life had to be lived with integrity, consistency and a servant heart.

As my time at Bible College came to an end, David Perry challenged me about the depth and breadth of the talents I wanted to use to serve God and the Church. He helped me to see that my ability to work effectively with church leaders would be weakened if I did not have any experience of pastoral ministry myself. I began to understand that I needed to be exposed to the many challenges of leadership and I felt that the Lord was confirming this direction. This led to me taking responsibility for the church I was attending in south London, in the capacity of leading elder, a role for which I initially felt unprepared, and in which I had to negotiate around my own naivety along a path marked by conflict and scepticism. By God's grace I was able to work with that church and its denomination for eight years, and over that time I was able to establish my own vision for the place of evangelism in the life of the church as I led the congregation to be a catalyst for social action in its community.

I believe that evangelism is not a secondary phase of church ministry – something that can be addressed when other departments or functions are running smoothly. For me, all parts of church life are facilitated by evangelism. It's not a fringe activity or a luxury add-on. Evangelism is at the heart of a change in attitude to the life of the church. I led the church with the vision that it was outreach that would make other parts of the church healthy and fruitful, not the other way around.

Culture clash

In the late 1980s I met Simon Thomas. He describes me as someone 'wandering around telling his story', and I'm grateful to God that I was able to keep wandering with him. When I first got to know Simon, he was teaching at a secondary school in Kent but working with inner city kids as well. In his life as in mine, God had been stirring thoughts about the compartments of 'white' and 'black' Christians and 'white' and 'black' church leaders. We both could see that there was a strong tendency for white Christians to follow white leaders and black Christians to follow black leaders. Just as I had pushed these boundaries with Andrew Brandon a few years earlier, Simon was another individual who was not afraid of a culture clash, and who, with the power of the Holy Spirit, wanted to break some of the moulds that shaped church life and community life.

Simon invited me to lead a Year 11 assembly at his school. I took along my biography *Dreadlocks*, which had recently been published, and spoke about my youth and how my life had been changed by God. It was a winner – I was truly able to connect with those young people. The majority of pupils at the school were white, and through that assembly God opened my eyes once again to the possibilities and purposes he might have for a black man engaging with white youths. So began a period of experimentation in which Simon and I worked with groups and individuals desperately needing to reconnect with society, for which the multicultural mix of our partnership and our desire to keep breaking the mould of what was culturally acceptable was a blessed tool. As I got to know Simon better, I came to appreciate his great mind and his gift of communication. He says he 'took a risk with me' and I came to think of him as another David of the Old Testament – small but packing a powerful punch.

In the late 1980s, as Simon took up a team leader's role with Ichthus Christian Fellowship, and as I continued to lead my church in south London, we travelled around the country leading church and community events. We were interested in breaking the insularity of the white Church/black Church divide. If we couldn't crack true fellowship in the Church, we figured, how could we crack it in the community? We were trying to bridge different elements of communities, by being a community in microcosm ourselves, rather than simply talking about it. We both believed that in ethnically diverse areas you can't just talk about multiculturalism – you have to do it and be it. That shows itself in the way we live: often the small ways in which we co-exist and share a street, a school, an environment. Some years later we gave what we were doing the informal name 'Culture Clash'.

'Community' is a buzzword now, a marketing hook, a politically expedient term, an aspiration. Back then, the word didn't have the same appeal. But we were always thinking about community. I think that what we knew of the Church's potential to be a community kept us pushing away at the communities outside it, as well as at the interface between Church and community. We have the picture of the Church as a body in the New Testament, with its interdependent parts, its protection for the weak, the equal concern for the different limbs (1 Corinthians). It's a picture of unity and diversity. But it wasn't enough to pray and talk about how our Christian communities could function better. We needed to ask, how is the function of a church community affected by the function of the 'real' community around it? How could we say that we were a true community of worshippers when we were not engaging with the people walking by outside the door? It could never be just a question of how do we do 'community' inside church. Christians needed to take themselves and the love of God outside and make it real. Communities needed to know that we were there. When we did this, we believed, communities would connect and influence each other and, we prayed, be blessed.

We took our events to many different venues, some quite large, like The Fridge nightclub in Brixton, south London. We would have music from a variety of bands, we would share a few stories. It was a combination of innovation, simplicity and song. Simple things are the most powerful. It allowed for the mixing of cultures to be interpreted in several ways: between Christian and secular, between black and white, between Christian music and secular music. We found that many Christians and many churches were already aware that people in their neighbourhood were not doing well: families and individuals were living with crime, poverty, the grief of seeing young lives lost in gang-related violence, the power of addiction, the brokenness of children left behind by a parent. The early 1990s marked the beginning of an awakening for me about the devastation that could be caused by guns, drugs and violence. There was a lot for me to learn, but I had already witnessed how much a community of people could 'know' about itself, its triumphs, its limits, its place in the structures of power. I saw that there could be communities within communities – not geographical communities, but what Simon Thomas calls 'communities of pain', lives that are bound together, people who are able to relate to each other – particularly as a result of gang and gun crime – and these were communities that were global as well as local. I was opening myself up to people who felt helpless and hopeless, as well as those who carried hopefulness inside them – hope that grew through interaction with places as they were right now, not that waited until they were the places we wanted them to be.

@CaroSwannie
V impressed with @StreetPastors training so far. Can't wait 4 next wk with Simon Thomas, a small man with a big personality

As a trainer on the first Street Pastors training programme, and over the years since then, Simon Thomas has helped many trainees to understand the relationship between Christianity and contemporary culture. Here he recounts the 'big desire' he and Les Isaac share to work in communities and see change, and describes the innovations they embarked on in the late 1980s and early 1990s.

Les Isaac comes from a very different background to me, but both of us have got a big desire to work in communities and see change. Over the years we've come at it from lots of different angles, and done lots of creative things together.

I've always been a teacher, but about twenty-five years ago I began to feel that, as a caring professional, part of a network of other professionals, I was fighting a losing battle with regard to the educational and social outcomes for my students. My attention was drawn to what was happening for kids when they left school at 3 p.m., given that it was very likely there would be no parent or carer around for them until 6 p.m. I worked with Southwark Council for a while, making suggestions, hanging out on the school buses, doing things with young people after school.

I was used to innovating ways to engage with people, to bring communities together, and after a while I said to a bunch of guys in my church, 'We're going to experiment.' My idea was that as Peckham, where I live, has got loads of nightclubs (lots of them with big reputations), we should hang out on the streets outside the clubs. It was very simple. We put out a table, got a stack of cards, printed them up with some nice artwork on the front and the words 'Restorer of streets with dwellings' on the back. It is a single sentence from the Old Testament book of Isaiah, significant words that God had inspired many of us with at that time. Over the months people had been praying, others had been talking to the police (Matt Baggott was Commissioner of Police in the borough at the time) and building up a picture of the needs of the area, but in the end we knew we actually had to get onto the streets.

We surprised a lot of people! Some assumed we were street cleaners, others that we were repairing street lights. We would walk up and down, chat, hang out, get people used to our faces, because we knew we were going to be back. Les came down to see what we were up to, with a couple of other church leaders.

Over the first few nights we got to know all the bouncers. When the door staff asked who we were, we said we were local pastors. One time we were invited to meet the manager of the club and escorted upstairs. He gave us free tickets, and said we were welcome to come there anytime we wanted. He said, 'So you are the Church are you?' Yes, we nodded. 'So why have you never been here before?'

That got us thinking a whole stack of things. We started to gather information about community engagement and a local youth organisation that we worked with surveyed about 1,000 local residents. We discovered two things: (1) young people feel afraid when they go out at night. Why? Because, they said, there were very few older people around to make them feel safe; (2) older people feel afraid when they go out at night. Why? Because there are too many young people around.

We knew we just had to be on the streets – not doing lots, but just being there. One young girl asked if she could hang out with us and I asked why she wanted to do that. The reason she gave was because she felt safer being with us while she waited for her bus. We had a feeling that we could change a dynamic. The area felt more peaceful and we wanted to keep that going.

For us, going out onto the streets was the natural way to develop what we had been praying and talking about. And, I believe, it is the Church's first responsibility to bring peace. When they appear to the shepherds in the fields, the angels say 'Glory to God in the highest heaven, and on earth peace'. I see this as Jesus' first announcement to earth! It's a difficult peace to get: it requires us to dig in, to break down walls and barriers. It's easy to miss what Jesus says about peace, but we must start with peace – 'Peace I leave with you; my peace I give you' – you have to start with this.

FAQ

How can I reach people with God's love?

Get out into your community. It's not rocket science. Jesus walked everywhere or travelled on a donkey; we have to rediscover walking around our communities. You could cycle, you could take the bus. I'm not going to tell you how to do evangelism, just get out there.

Les, CEO Ascension Trust

4

1990–2003:
Reality and response

....

I love travelling. I love the challenge of the unknown and I love meeting people. I don't always have to get my passport out – I love it when people travel to me and bring me news and views from other places. Being in a new place gives me the opportunity to learn about the way other people do things and observe what works for them in their context. For me this is a naturally slippery process, with lots of movement back and forth, from home to away and back again. I'll think about the context for my own role and responsibilities at home and I often find that I'm asking myself the question, 'How would this way of doing things work in my context?' Watching the way that life is lived in another country helps me to get a sharper understanding of the context at home that I am familiar with. I get a new perspective on the things that I've been doing – it's like looking up from a close study of the grass to focus in on a dandelion. So when I travel I'm unofficially on the lookout for what I can take away.

I've been privileged to experience other countries and cultures and, specifically, to get myself among people who are trying to do similar things to me with hearts that beat, like mine, for the same people groups and the same troubles. The first of these times of fertilisation came in 1992, not through a journey of my own, but from welcoming to London two ministers from the Episcopalian Church in Pennsylvania in the United States. I was told that they had insight and experience of drugs, guns and gangs in the States and, with my background, I was interested to hear what they had to say. During our conversations the pastors made plain to me the devastation caused to communities by guns and drugs and the high levels of violence associated with them. But these men had a lot more to lay at my doorstep than these horrifying stories. One of their purposes in coming to Britain was to hold meetings with our police service and local government officers in locations around the country to encourage them not to be complacent about these social issues. When I pressed them to say what kind of response they had received, they told me that they had been courteously received but reassured that the problems they had described were American problems. Local councils and police officers, the pastors reported, had been as lethargic as each other.

Towards the end of 1993, I joined Ichthus Christian Fellowship, a network of 'new' churches across south London, as the leader of the congregation in Crystal Palace. It was wonderful to be accepted into the Ichthus leadership team and know the assurance of being among people who loved and valued me. It was like coming home to a family! A few years earlier, Ichthus, together with other leaders and Christian movements, had initiated what became known (over the fourteen years of its lifetime) as the March for Jesus, an interdenominational event in which Christians marched through towns and cities proclaiming the good news of Jesus. Ichthus had clear views about making a public impact, especially in areas where they were planting a new church, and I joined wholeheartedly in these times of public worship. The March for Jesus was an example of how the initiatives coming from other Christian leaders at the time coincided with my own God-inspired desires. Those incredible days of the March for Jesus and the presence of thousands of Christians from all denominations on the streets of our major cities was part of a new prayerful engagement with cities and civic authorities. A candlelit prayer walk to Scotland Yard that took place just after I joined the Ichthus leadership was another expression of this. Around this time, the Ichthus leadership team also invited officers from the Metropolitan Police to one of our celebration services at South Street Baptist Church in Greenwich so that we could pray for them and hear about the challenges they faced. The role of the Christian Police Association (CPA) in brokering new levels of trust between the police and communities and churches is described more fully in Chapter 6.

And so I began to get a sense of my own calling. There was overlap between me and the missional message coming from Ichthus, but there was a weight in my own spirit as my own distinct vision began to form.

Ascension Trust was the first expression of that vision. I founded the charity in 1993, with the purpose of empowering churches and individuals to be effective in cross-cultural, urban outreach. At first it primarily, but not exclusively, targeted African and Caribbean churches. At this grass-roots level I was getting exposure to the issues that were troubling communities. Though I was collecting information about things that were happening in other countries, and my radar was beginning to tune in to accounts of drug-related violence in UK cities, I wasn't yet sure what kind of response to make.

However, these things sometimes have a life of their own and, as a community leader and church minister, I began to be invited to give statements and opinions in the press about young people, rising street crime and gang cultures. I gave an interview to the *Voice* newspaper and took part in several radio broadcasts, expressing my concerns about these matters. As my voice began to be heard, so Ascension Trust's credibility grew, and we began to be seen as a source of a grass-roots response to the issues. Public questions and political interest were growing around the subject of gun ownership, and in 1996 the Cullen Inquiry drew a link between gun ownership and crime in the wake of the Dunblane massacre. The warnings that I had received from the two American pastors some years previously (that what we were seeing in the UK was only the 'tip of the iceberg') returned to me as I began to get a sense of how violent and gun-related crime can be both the cause and the symptom of other social fractures beneath the waterline: lack of opportunity, low educational achievement, fatherless families, poor housing, conflict between communities and the police.

I approached Ascension Trust's board of trustees with the message that we were ideally placed to respond to the issues of drugs, guns and gangs, headed as we were by myself, a black Caribbean man, and closer than many other organisations to the dynamics of an issue that was, at that time, largely focused on the Caribbean community. The conclusion we reached was that we needed to get an up-to-date picture of the situation. We needed to consult and to analyse.

In 2000 I got to know Bobby Wilmot, the pastor of a church in a deprived area of Kingston, Jamaica, who had read my *Dreadlocks* biography and wanted to share with me some of his experiences of living and leading a church in a community that was ravaged by gun crime and gang violence. Over the years this initial contact has grown wonderfully into a partnership between Ascension Trust and Operation Save Jamaica that encapsulates expertise and solutions but, most of all, the inspirational value of 'seeing for yourself'. As Pastor Bobby puts it, we are taught to 'Come and see' by Jesus, who answered a question from his disciples about where he was living with the words, 'Come . . . and you will see' (John 1:39). Instead of a verbal description about the place, the disciples got to spend the day there with Jesus. With this as part of our rationale, delegations from Jamaica and England have visited each other's countries over the years.

Back then, at our first meeting, my heart leapt as I heard Pastor Bobby talk about a country I only knew from reggae artists and their music. He spoke of the exciting alliance between his downtown congregation and churches from an 'uptown' part of the city which, together, had set up training and job schemes and a school in Rema, Trench Town. Bobby and the pastor of one of the uptown churches, Bruce Fletcher, had demonstrated extraordinary commitment to serve a ravaged community. It was time for me to learn from these inspiring partnerships, to see the devastation and meet the victims of this Jamaica for myself.

Kingston

My opportunity came following a mission I was leading in St Vincent and Guyana in the Caribbean. The father of one of my co-leaders died, and I detoured with her to Jamaica to visit her family. As we approached the island from the air, I could see the grandeur of white-painted mansions backed by the Blue Mountains. It wasn't as easy to pick out the squalid shanty-towns that I knew were just a short drive away from the prestigious Beverly Hills area. I was heading for a place that mixed tourism with homicide. In 2002 the homicide rate reached 40 per 100,000 people, the third highest in the world.

Bobby Wilmot met me in Kingston and over the coming days he guided me around his neighbourhood, Trench Town. I was struck by the intensity of the aggression as I walked around this area, negotiating burnt-out cars, fridges and other large objects that had been deliberately left in the road to make drive-by shootings less easy. Policemen and soldiers patrolled in open-top jeeps, all fully armed themselves. I was amazed by the tremendous work that the alliance of churches had managed to achieve in Trench Town. The funds had been hard to come by, but they had eventually been able to convert disused communal shower and toilet facilities into a school-room. I met children who were enjoying going to school but heard from their teachers of the great challenge of educating these kids and being involved with their families at the same time as the long fingers of local gangs snaked into every corner of family life. The children's older siblings (only nine or ten years old themselves) were being groomed to be gang recruits and use guns. Uncles and brothers were in the gang, as was their mother's boyfriend. I saw how impossible it was to live in that community without being affected by gangs and guns.

So what could I do with this awful truth? How would the Jamaican context shape my understanding of the British context? I was now fully awake to the potentially serious problems in my home city and other British cities. I was clear about what I had learned, but could I clearly communicate that to others?

Some things were certain. That antisocial behaviour escalates into more serious, violent crime was the first thing of which I was sure. Intimidation, joyriding, carjacking, vandalism and drunkenness already caused distress and fear in many communities, and their potential to be driven to another level by drug- and gang-related triggers was high. That two-way information-gathering process was at work again when, with the backing of Ichthus leaders, I invited pastors Bobby Wilmot and Bruce Fletcher to come to London and talk with church and community leaders about the realities of guns, drugs and gangs. I needed to raise the finances to make this possible and to make the discussion mobile. I was planning, in effect, a roadshow that would be able to visit different locations around London and other major cities as well. My aim was to talk, share experiences, listen and take soundings on public feeling.

Guns on our streets

The 'Guns on our streets' tour was the consultation vehicle that took to the roads in 2002 and eventually led to the 'Guns off our streets' report, which was presented to Ascension Trust trustees. The trust didn't work alone in this. I had discovered that a member of the Ichthus congregation in Forest Hill worked for the Metropolitan Police's special unit that dealt with gun crimes within London's black community, known as Operation Trident. I met this officer and spoke to him of our desire to work with and support the police. That officer went back to his bosses and put us in touch with each other. Trident's mandate fitted exactly with the things we were seeking to understand, and we were very pleased to be able to organise the 'Guns on our streets' presentations and receptions in conjunction with Operation Trident. This was the beginning of a relationship with the Metropolitan Police Service that, as time went by, became fundamental to the operational success of Street Pastors. The Met was tentatively starting to look outside its own institution for ways of tackling urban problems, so when we came to them and asked, 'Can you use us?', there was some willingness to involve us and a recognition that we could be part of the solution.

Detective Ian Crichlow, one of the Trident superintendents, was seconded to us for a week so that he could be a part of the tour. He played a key role both in that week and subsequently, as our aims and vision developed. He spoke to audiences and presented information about gun crime in London and the rapid increase in gun ownership. DC Crichlow told us that in the year 2001–02, gun crimes had tripled in the capital. In the period from January to August 2002, and compared to the same period the year before, murders were up by 14 per cent, attempted murders had increased by 8 per cent and other shooting incidents had risen by 98 per cent, from 43 incidents to 85 incidents.

Bobby Wilmot and Bruce Fletcher described how churches in Kingston had begun to engage with people affected by or caught up in gun crime, and how churches had a responsibility to interact with those individuals. Pastor Bobby described how when the call to action was initially sounded in Kingston, it fell on deaf ears – until two things happened. First, the middle-class families of the 'uptown' districts realised that their own sons and daughters were caught up in gangs and gun crime. Second, when churches began to campaign and invited their members to Trench Town to see for themselves what life was like there, those church members understood so much more than what the television news had told them. Many of them had left Trench Town thirty years before and sworn never to go back, but when they were persuaded to actually walk Trench Town's streets, they were stirred up to take some responsibility for that neighbourhood. The message from Jamaica was that when too many people say, 'I'll stay in my small corner, and you stay in yours', communities disintegrate. Those that are outside the problem must not, Bobby Wilmot and Bruce Fletcher told us, abandon the community, no matter how bad things are. Our presence, our interest, our interaction are important factors in transformation.

Now, working in close partnership with DC Crichlow and the Trident team, our thinking and planning was shaped further by David Shosanya's visit to Boston in the United States. David was a trustee of Ascension Trust and, at the time, pastor of Chalk Farm Baptist Church in north London, though he was soon to become Regional Minister for Mission in London for the Baptist Association. In Boston David saw how churches had responded, in obedience to the Bible's teaching, to young gang members. A group of local church ministers had taken seriously the invitation to reconciliation as an integral part of Christian worship. In the New Testament, Jesus teaches that if, as you approach the altar in worship, you remember that 'your brother or sister has something against you', you are to leave your gift and seek reconciliation with your brother or sister (Matthew 5:23–4). The Boston pastors knew that although, on the face of things, it appeared that aggressive gang members were the ones who needed to make reparation, there were many ways in which the disenfranchisement of these young men from community life was something for which the community should also take responsibility. In the eyes of the gang members, David told us, 'the community has committed an offence against them'.

The church leaders resolved to make themselves available to talk to these young people and formed a 'Ten-point coalition' to outline their determination for on the-street, face-to-face connection. My heart lurched as I listened to David describe how he had seen for himself a new, grass-roots response from the gang members to the wider community that was repre sented by the church leaders. It was time to publicise the 'Guns on our streets' tour and get the word out to local government chief executives, probation officers, social workers, police officers, community leaders, church leaders and parents. We planned to visit five London boroughs, and then move on to Birmingham and then Moss Side and Longsight in Manchester. The pattern we thought best was a lunchtime reception or civic meeting for invited guests, and then an evening meeting open to the general public.

I, DC Crichlow, David Shosanya, Bobby Wilmot and Bruce Fletcher gave presentations about the reality of gun ownership in inner cities, graphically illustrated by police footage of crime scenes and distraught victims, and we spoke about the environment that had developed in Jamaica. Our message was clear: the situation is urgent and all parts of the community must engage with the young men involved in gun crime.

The urban trinity

The key point of Pastor Wilmot's message to the 'Guns on our streets' audience was that one entity alone cannot tackle the problem of gun- and gang-related crime; one entity on its own, by definition, cannot achieve a 'community' response or consider itself to represent a district or a neighbourhood. Apart from the limitations of any one sector's response, I asked myself: did I know many Christians who would know what to do if someone handed them a gun or a knife to get it out of harm's way? Would they know what to do if an individual said, 'I want to get out of my gang'? Likewise, I thought, do the other big players in our cities and towns think of Christians as a potential resource? Have they noticed that we have churches on virtually every high street in this country? So through the 'Guns on the street' tour, we said to all possible partners, 'Let's help each other. Let's understand where each other is coming from.'

It was for these reasons – the enormous potential and the evident limitations of one sector on its own – that we argued that the Church needed to be in partnership with other community agencies. We were convinced that the three biggest structures in any city when it comes to power and resources are the local government, the police and the Church. You can read more about these partnerships in Part 3. My vision was for all three to complement and support each other for the benefit of the community.

The response we received during the tour was mixed, generally a few degrees either side of lukewarm. The finer details of the reservations held by groups on all sides became apparent in time, but as things stood during the months that we toured London, Birmingham and Manchester, the main components of the scepticism that I came across were: prejudice towards Christianity; filing away the issue as 'ethnic' rather than societal; the risk that Christians would preach rather than be practical; safety concerns; fears that whoever went out in the front line would not be accepted by young people on the street; and the belief that the problems of gun and knife crime were only found in isolated pockets. There was uncertainty about what to do coupled with a reluctance to face up to reality.

There was no hope of the Catholic Church or the Church of England picking up the issue. I'd had no response from the former, and all I was offered by the latter was a slot on the agenda of the next synod in two years' time! Over time I met with other denominational leaders, all the while sending out letters to church leaders informing them of the information that had been gathered via the roadshow, with the message that this issue should not be swept under carpet or labelled 'black' or 'urban'. Gun and knife crime has the potential to impact all of us, I wrote, and we need all traditions of the Church to get on board because of the enormity of the problem. It was important not just to fire off some soundbites about the urgency of the situation, but to encourage churches to reflect on their role in the community, to examine how they used their buildings and resources, to look into the Bible's teaching about being 'salt and light' to the world. A small number of church leaders replied to me and some admitted that they hadn't got a theological or practical response to the needs of their community. In general the response to my letters and phone calls at this time was disappointing. It confirmed what I knew already: that there was a tendency to think that this was someone else's problem; and that the thought of working with the police and local councils filled church leaders with uncertainty. The cautiousness meant that access to the initiative for the person in the pew was going to be limited.

Those few church leaders who came to the reception that we hosted in Brixton Baptist Church towards the end of 2002 were, as Roger Forster, the leader of Ichthus Christian Fellowship, remembers, 'half converted' to the idea already. I remember listening to Roger's inspirational talk and feeling that, though this was a slow start, it was a start nonetheless: a small number of churches were coming together to do something about the problems facing their neighbourhoods. Some church leaders were delighted to be at that reception; others were just plain relieved that someone else had stuck their head above the parapet.

Although it was not all positive, we learned an enormous amount from the roadshow and the attempts at connecting with churches and leaders in the months that followed. A spin-off meeting with the borough commander for Lambeth, Chief Superintendent Dick Quinn, led us to two important discoveries. When I asked him about how the challenges for his officers fluctuated or peaked during the day, his answer was very informative. He told me that two sections of the day were critical in terms of policing: the first was in the afternoon between 2 p.m. and 6 p.m. Between these hours, children and young people come out of school and college, and this often caused disturbances and a level of fear in residents and shopping areas, where it was felt that the young people were unproductively killing time. The second key time was triggered by activity around pubs and clubs, particularly when pubs close and people move onto clubs, and when the clubs themselves close up. He referred to the four hours between 11 p.m. and 3 a.m. As a teenager I had opted for an alternative life-style out of anger and exclusion, and now, here I was, finding myself drawing nearer to this world again. Just like Simon Thomas, who had believed that 'hanging out' around the clubs and pubs was the right way to introduce himself to the Peckham street scene, I and others from Ascension Trust began to walk around our localities at night to get a feel for what was going on. We were starting to see that the work God was calling us to do would not be done inside one of 'our' venues, but on the streets at night.

A tragic catalyst for change

On New Year's Day 2003, my wife, Louise, and I spent the day with my in-laws, as we did every New Year. It was our habit to pray together as a family, to reflect on the past year and give thanks for it. I remember feeling a heaviness in my heart for young people, and I presented my hopes and fears for this generation in prayer. I prayed, 'Lord, the Church has not fully grasped the magnitude of the problem.'

The following day, concerns about young people and society were not just voiced in my in-laws' front room, but in front rooms up and down the country. On 2 January, every news channel carried headlines about the shooting of four young girls, two fatally, in Aston, Birmingham. My phone was ringing like crazy with journalists asking questions, and church leaders suddenly making renewed connections between the message of the roadshow and the tragedy of lives lost. For some, it was as simple as that: they connected what we had presented, what we were planning and what we had prayed about with the reality of another person's life and death – young people at a party in a hairdresser's salon under a hail of bullets.

Calvin Young, pastor of Aston Christian Centre in Birmingham, found himself in the middle of a media storm. In our hurried phone calls, he apologised for the lack of interest among churches in his locality which, the year before, had not wanted to be part of the 'Guns on our streets' events. Everything that we had been talking about was suddenly front-page news, and I saw a wider group of people now starting to ask questions about drugs, guns and gangs. Local people in Aston were of one mind – there should be a major event to bring the community together, mark the loss of innocent life, and take a stand as strangers, neighbours, parents and children, against gang violence. Two weeks later, thousands of people flocked to Aston Villa football stadium for an excellent programme of musicians and speakers. The bishop of Birmingham was there, together with leaders from the Muslim and Hindu communities.

The Street Pastors initiative was launched just three weeks later in Brixton Baptist Church on 28 January. Pastor Calvin

Young from Aston spoke about the impact of gun crime on their community. Paul Keeble, who had been involved in the 'Gangstop' march in Manchester, reported on the picture in his city. Inspector Bob Pull from the Metropolitan Police gave the police perspective. Roger Forster shared a reflection on the need for a Christian-led response. There was a big turnout. In this new atmosphere, it was being said that something must be done. Now there was a willingness to join where someone else was paving the way. As Roger Forster remembers it, anticipation was in the air.

I laid out the proposal and the concept for Street Pastors. My emphasis was on the fact that we must do something because we have the grace, power, conviction and love of our Lord Jesus Christ. If there were murmurs of 'ambitious', I said, 'We need ambitious people!' I endeavoured not to make Street Pastors sound like another mission, and I think this shift away from the traditional framework for outreach made it difficult for some church leaders to see their role in Street Pastors. On the one hand, those that I would have assumed least likely to get involved – some retired and senior folk – were beginning to express an interest in Street Pastors, and on the other, it was clear that many still had unanswered questions.

Roger Forster recalls how we 'sold' the idea of Street Pastors in the context of the fears and questions that were raised, by reminding people that if we take too much notice of negativity we will forget that we are people of faith, meant to live by faith. When we heard the question, 'Is it safe to walk the streets at night?', we redirected big fears towards small actions. We said, 'It is only showing a bit of love on the streets . . . we can do that.' We were not being reckless or dismissive. In truth, the Street Pastors initiative was about small, simple and genuine interventions in the lives of the people around us.

Core values

The 'Guns on our streets' tour produced a lot of information and feedback that DC Ian Crichlow, David Shosanya and I were committed to acting on rather than archiving. At the launch event in January 2003 we made it clear that our response to the scoping exercises of 2002 was to ask the Church to work in partnership with the police and local government structures, and to go out onto the streets at night to connect with and care for the individuals they met. Together we formed a list of core values that would underpin our proposals, and which became fundamental to the 'Guns off our streets' report that we circulated.

The core values of Street Pastors
- A belief in the sacredness and sanctity of human life;
- The importance of valuing and honouring our community, and taking pride in the place where we live;
- The development of integrity. Integrity is a vital part of the fabric of society;
- The desire to take personal responsibility. We can express this in our own relationships and 'niche' in a network or community, and we can encourage others to understand that they do not have to become victims of their own circumstances;
- The development of individuals to their fullest potential. We believe that each individual can make a major contribution to society. Other people can help that awareness to grow.

As we wrote in the 'Guns off our streets' report, these statements connect us to the teachings of our Christian faith, to universally upheld values and to African and Caribbean history. Honouring and valuing community is rooted in the African concept of *ubuntu*, which says, 'I am only a person through other persons.'

We also turned our attention to the name we should give ourselves and anyone else who joined us. There were two main things to note: first, streets full of problems and, second, people needing someone to care for them and demonstrate hope to them. The word pastor was suggested not in the sense of ordination, but in its literal meaning, 'shepherd', 'carer'. From there it was a small step to the name 'street pastor'.

The first night

The name we had chosen for the initiative and our volunteers was questioned a great deal in the early days of our work. Some thought it was too 'churchy' or too 'in your face'. But it was a God-given tool for breaking the ice with people. And then, as now, it perfectly describes who we are! I was worried, as were others in the small, brave group that walked around Brixton on our first official night out, that there wouldn't be any understanding of what we were doing. The tremendous sense of occasion that I felt as I put on my new uniform did battle with some unnerving questions. 'Would we be welcomed?' 'Would we be ignored?' 'What if something went wrong?' Now was the time to find out what kind of interaction God had in store for us.

I'll always remember how, that night, we were acknowledged and recognised as Christian men and women. It was not because we kept reminding people of it, but because of the bold letters printed across the back of our coats: PASTOR. Most people we met that night understood the connection between that word and the Church. People hugged us, purely because they were happy to see us and because, as they made clear, 'it was about time' that the Church came out of its building! I was so excited! I thought. 'Wow, they get it!' The general public seemed to implicitly understand that on the streets was where the Church should be. I heard people saying it all night long.

We headed for a known drug-dealing patch and, as we approached, we saw groups of dealers, maybe eight of them in all, spread out with about twenty-five metres between each of them. There was a brisk trade going on, with people pulling up in their cars all the time. We simply said, 'Good evening', and continued our walk. One of the dealers, however, looked up and said, 'Pastor, will you pray for me? I need prayer.' There it was – the connection to the word 'Pastor' and a readiness to engage with people of peace. Of course, it wasn't easy to pray for a drug dealer! My heart raced. What should I pray for, I wondered? I can't pray God's blessing on his business, that's for sure! I asked God for the words. I was just about to open my mouth when a man walked up to the dealer, fingering a wad of notes in his hand. The dealer turned to him and said, 'Go away. I'm having the pastor pray for me. Come back later.' Then I prayed for God's help for this man, to give him a sense of purpose and lead him in the path of righteousness. He said a loud 'Amen' and sincerely thanked me.

As we walked on we introduced ourselves to door staff, shop owners, pub landlords. I talked to one young man, as he leaned out of his car window to get a better look at us. I asked him what he thought about young people carrying guns. 'I carry a gun,' he said, pointing to the glove compartment. 'If I didn't, people would take advantage of me. I've even given my mother a can of CS gas in case she is attacked.' I was amazed at the ease with which he spoke. He was simply saying, 'This is the way things are.' As he wound up his window, he added, 'You've got a big job on your hands.'

Sharon and Eustace Constance were part of the first group of street pastors that took to the streets of Brixton on a Friday night in April 2003. That night there were eighteen volunteers altogether: fifteen women and three men, plus a BBC cameraman.

Eustace: Most of the first group would have had some contact with Ascension Trust before they became a street pastor, most likely through a presentation at their church about Street Pastors, or through their general awareness of the trust as a charity that led overseas missions and youth missions and delivered training. That was my experience. In 2003 I had already been on several missions with Ascension Trust and was a member of its board of trustees. At the time that I signed up to be in the first batch of Street Pastors trainees, I was working for Islington Borough Council, but not long after this I became the first Street Pastors area co-ordinator for the borough of Lewisham. Subsequently I became co-ordinator for Hackney and then Operations Manager for Ascension Trust and Street Pastors, a job I've done for five years now.

Sharon: My contact with Ascension Trust also predated Street Pastors, as I was already helping with its administration when I put myself forward to be in the first group of trainees. My full-time job was working as a quality assurance manager at East Thames Housing Association.

Eustace: We were all strangers at the beginning, not quite sure what it would be like to go out and minister with each other. The group was predominantly women. The gender ratio was a bit of a concern, though, as we were going to Brixton. I would have felt more comfortable if we had had more men. I always hoped and prayed that more men would come, and they did, after the first couple of years. I asked God, and others were asking too, where are your men? But God's plan and our plan will always be different. We've learned the effectiveness of women.

Sharon: The training was very good. It covered what we could expect when we went out, the purpose of us going out, what we would do when we got there. I found it empowering.

Eustace: I recall that on the first night we communicated the vision for Street Pastors. There weren't any stories or experiences to share like there are now. At that time it was a story of how we had got to that point. Les's visit to Jamaica was talked about, as well as

David Shosanya's experiences in the USA. There was a lot to say to explain the reasoning for Street Pastors. If we hadn't done that with the first trainees it would have been like starting a conversation halfway through.

Sharon: On that first night out, I felt a lot of apprehension and fear mixed with excitement. Do you remember how some of the group felt sick? Once I got outside and started walking and talking to people I felt totally secure. The briefing took place at the office on Overton Road, and when we left there we walked through the Angell Town estate and towards Brixton. Then we split into three groups, with one group heading into the centre of Brixton, one turning right at the police station and the other group making their way towards the town hall. We didn't have any radios, because that would have associated us too much with the police. We used our mobile phones instead to keep in touch.

Eustace: In the weeks preceding that night, the media had been asking pertinent questions about what we would be doing, whether we would be preaching or spoiling people's fun. We weren't at all sure what sort of response we would get.

Sharon: There was one man who said, 'You're too late, the horse has bolted.' And we sensed the sadness that some people had. Do you remember the chip-shop owner? He told us that he was selling his business – directly opposite Brixton Police Station – because so many girls had run into his shop shouting that they had been attacked or raped. He couldn't take it any more.

Eustace: Yes, he wished us well but he believed that we were too little, too late. One of our aims was to say 'Hello' to all the local businesses and takeaways, and when we went into that chip shop, the proprietor asked his assistant to carry on serving and we had a lengthy conversation.

Sharon: Which resulted in you getting a portion of chips.

Eustace: This is true. But this man had lost hope, though he really wanted to see things differently. He told me about the many times people had used his shop as a refuge. Once he had taken a girl *inside because she said she was the victim of an attempted rape, and then he had made sure she got safely home. He said, 'I've lived here for 30 years, but I don't recognise this place any more.'*

Sharon: We wanted to make a connection with people. We knew that when we went out we could be, at any given time, not far away from a tragic event. I don't mean that we feared for our safety, but that we were aware that we would meet people whose lives were blighted by grief, anger, fear or loss. We reckoned we could make things better and that night confirmed to us that people were looking for a glue to bind the community together.

Eustace: We agreed to return to Overton Road after two-and-a-half hours. I've yet to go out with a team on their first night that gets back on time! When we were all assembled again for a debriefing, the story was the same for all three teams: the first reaction we'd had was one of welcome, with people being excited to see us; the second reaction was formed as a question – would we be back or were we a flash in the pan?

Sharon: Yes, I heard people say, 'You're the Church? You'll be gone in a couple of weeks.' I stressed that we were here for the long term. We really didn't want to be seen as the kind of people that would be standing around a Christmas tree in December or giving out tracts at Easter. We wanted people to see us every weekend. So after that first patrol in Brixton we decided to go out again the following night in Hackney.

Eustace: We wanted to see if what had happened the night before was just a Brixton thing, or whether it would be repeated. And when we arrived in Hackney one of the first people we met was a lady coming out of a hairdresser's on Kingston High Road. She had been at a funeral that morning and had heard talk about Street Pastors. She told us that she had prayed at the graveside, 'Lord, let them come to Hackney.'

I was no stranger to outreach but being a street pastor was something completely different. With the Street Pastors uniform on, people engaged with us and we didn't come across as a group of strange people; I found that the uniform communicated a level of organisation, so people were more at ease. They were at ease because they could make the approach to us. I can remember it like it was yesterday, because since then I've been to lots of 'first nights' with teams from all over the country, and the same things happen wherever Street Pastors is launched. It keeps the memory of the very first patrol fresh for me.

FAQ

Why do Christians sometimes debate whether 'words' or 'actions' are more important to the presentation of the message of Jesus?

That question takes me back a long way. I remember that it was not uncommon to hear Christians saying, 'We are here to preach and pray. Is it right to invest all this energy in new projects?' or, 'Doesn't putting emphasis on social action take the edge off preaching the gospel?' Serving people, at that time, wasn't in the picture. In the recent history of the public face of Christianity, this meant that those who called themselves 'liberals' took the practical expression (actions) of the gospel of Jesus out of the hands of the evangelicals. By the same token, forty years ago, evangelicals let go of social initiatives, considering them to be wrong because they detracted from the Church's ability to preach the gospel (words). The movement in these positions that has taken place over my ministerial lifetime is colossal, with biblical Christians now being prepared to get involved in the 'liberal gospel'. Around the time that Street Pastors started up, things were beginning to change.

Roger, church leader

5

The night I met a street pastor: Sandy

....

Working on the doors of Stirling's pubs and clubs, Sandy was used to viewing the aggression and drunkenness on the streets of the city up close and personal. He had also battled his own issues with alcohol and violence over the years. As he saw it, his job as the company 'enforcer' was simply to remove anyone causing trouble as quickly and efficiently as possible, and not to think too hard about any consequences.

'For more than twenty years I worked as a bouncer (we call it "doorman") in the pubs and clubs of Stirling. It's an aggressive job. Clubs need someone like me on the front step because they don't want trouble inside the building. They want to make sure it can't get in. Like most doormen I was employed by a big company and sent to clubs in the city where they needed some special help. I would be in one place for about six weeks, clean it up a bit – get on top of any regular trouble, lay down the law – then someone else would take over.

'I had a bit of a reputation, I suppose. Most people knew I could only take so much. Folk knew that if they crossed the line, there would be consequences. I would say to trouble-makers, "You can go in, but if I have to come in and get you it's not going to be nice."

'In 2003 I moved to Belfast because my marriage had broken

down. Violence was part of my life there, too, as I was involved in the UVF as a paramilitary. When I came back to Stirling in 2009, I went straight back to working on the doors.

'I would be on the door all night, along with another guy, wrapped up warm as best we could. The critical time was usually around quarter to one when people were moving from bars to clubs. The nightlife in Stirling is not too bad compared to other places. The worst of it is that there are a lot of wee villages around about, and when those village folk come into town they are looking for fights with people from the other villages. They're always competing with each other.

'The first time I met the street pastors was the first night I was working after I had come back to Stirling. I wondered what they were. I thought to myself, what are these guys going to do? What's the good of preaching to people who are drunk? That's a pointless operation. I watched them walking around, talking to people, talking to doormen. Even though I was a bit uncertain about them, I welcomed them. There was no barrier between us. They were all friendly but I clicked with one of them in particular and, as we got talking, she explained what they were about and why they were there. Then I got to know James and he told me that all the street pastors are volunteers from different churches. Straight away, after these initial conversations, I started to change the way I thought about them. They presented themselves well.

'What I normally did with a troublemaker or someone who was really drunk was to throw them off the premises onto the pavement. Once they were gone, I wasn't bothered. I just wanted to get them out the door, and I didn't care what happened to them. Suddenly, as I got to know the street pastors, I found I had a conscience about this! It was because I knew that I could call on them, I think, that it helped me to think differently. You see, all the pubs and clubs and the street pastors, too, are linked by radio, and so when the street pastors were around I found myself calling them. I would tell them that I had thrown someone out, a girl or a lad who was very drunk, and ask them if they could come and see that they were all right. One time there was a lass who was very drunk. I couldn't have her on the premises because she was too far gone and she'd lost all her friends. I kept her next to me on the door and got the street pastors to come round and sort her out.

'God has always been round about, that's how I've thought of him. But I had never clearly thought about faith. About two or three weeks after I'd first met them, I told a street pastor called Maggie that the Jehovah's Witnesses had given me a Bible a long time ago, but the print was too small and I couldn't read it. One night Maggie came up to me and gave me a parcel. Inside was a large-print Bible. She said she'd been telling a local church about the work of Street Pastors and someone had given her £20 to go towards their work. She went out and bought me the Bible with it and suggested a couple of verses that I could read.

'Then there's James, the coordinator. I've met up with James for coffee quite a few times. Our friendship blossomed straight away from that first time we met. No, I'd never thought about faith up till then. I started to think about it because of my conversations with James and the other street pastors, and hearing James talk about his faith in God. That got me thinking. I just didn't like the lifestyle I was in and the violence and the things I got up to. James invited me to a church in the town; I enjoyed it but wanted to try another place. Soon after that I found a church that has become home for me, and after I'd been there a while I put my hand up at the end of the service when the pastor asked if anyone wanted to find out more about being a Christian. A few months later I was baptised.

'I've been on an addiction recovery programme run by a church in the town and I'm doing a lot of voluntary work for the Salvation Army and looking forward to becoming a full-time

Salvation Army soldier soon. I've trained as a chef and I run the soup kitchen for them, and I help out with their furniture warehouse. When I started to get involved with the church I was able to put words together better. The violent side of me has died down. In my younger days I was not patient. It's only recently that I've learned to tolerate people and give them a bit more leeway.'

PART THREE

Partnership

@ShirleyPolice
Lates team booked on, dealing with incidents, 3 Special
Constables working with us too & we're working with
@StreetPastors again tackling ASB

6

The wider policing family

....

This part of the book takes each element of what I refer to as the 'urban trinity' – the interrelated power structures in any town or city – and looks at how Street Pastors teams partner with each of them – the police, local authorities and the Church. I begin here with the police, with whom, after the launch in January 2003, our relationship began to take shape.

Apart from our connections to the Met's Trident unit and Detective Constable Ian Crichlow, we were greatly helped by Chief Inspector Leroy Logan (also chairman of the Black Police Association) and Inspector Bob Pull (then chairman of the Metropolitan Police branch of the Christian Police Association [CPA]), both of whom believed strongly in what we were doing. At this early stage, the police, and Christian police officers in particular, grasped the vision for Street Pastors in a much bigger and more assertive way than church leaders.

Involving Christians in the work of police officers and, vice versa, police officers in the life of churches was a concept that had already gained significant ground in south London by the time Street Pastors was being talked of. PC Andy Coles from the Brixton policing team and Reverend Ray Djan, the leader of the black majority True Vine Church in Brixton, first met at a police carol service in Brixton in 1996. PC Coles shared with the church leader his desire to start an outreach initiative in Brixton Police Station and asked if Reverend Djan would join him and a couple of other officers to pray. Ray Djan was keen to pray and, more than this, he told Andy Coles of a 'crazy idea' he'd had – that the police would alert churches to prayer needs and Christians would agree to pray for them.

'Adopt a Cop' was the name given to this idea and PC Coles wrote to all the churches in the Brixton area, inviting them into the partnership. Andy recalls the great response that the plan received from churches, leading him to work out a protocol for the sharing of information. 'There was a need for a degree of confidentiality,' he says. 'It was agreed that on our side we would only refer to officers by their initials or their first name only, and give brief details about the need for prayer, sometimes no details at all. Prayer requests were for individual officers and for issues in the local community.' When Andy Coles moved from Brixton to Wimbledon, he introduced Adopt a Cop at his new station. Shortly after this, he was invited to the national CPA conference, where he spoke about the initiative to members of the CPA from around the country. Adopt a Cop was adopted nationally by the CPA in 1999 to become a model that was available for other police forces to use.

The vision of Adopt a Cop was for police officers to be better integrated into their communities and for them to be seen as an element of the community that needed and welcomed support. Formerly mainly event-based in its approach to outreach, the CPA began to identify itself with developing relationships between police and faith communities. Andy Coles started to find that officers in the station at Brixton would ask for prayer and that local churches would invite officers to speak at church events. At this time, relationships between the police and churches took off most successfully in areas where there was most anti-police feeling, and took root most productively as black Christians in particular started to say 'enough is enough' with regard to hatred of the police. Those who genuinely believed that the police were not as bad as they were perceived to be wanted to see a healthier relationship take shape. Likewise, there were Christian officers who were wondering how they could prove that the police service was better than many thought it was.

Confidence slowly grew in the idea. There was plenty of cynicism in the Brixton policing team but, by and large, Adopt a Cop grabbed quite a bit of attention. Once officers realised that information wasn't being released recklessly, and Christians got used to this new type of engagement, Adopt a Cop was accepted on both sides.

Insp_AlexR

I've been giving a talk to #StreetPastors in #Lymington this evening. A very enthusiastic group who are going to make a real difference

Through Adopt a Cop, churches signed up to pray for officers, which often led to positive bridge-building and sometimes practical support; for example, local churches gathered around to help after the Brixton nail bombing in April 1999, many of them making their premises available to the police. There were other practical expressions of the new relationship. Church ministers went to the bedside of a seriously injured officer to pray for him. Andy Coles recalls how Adopt a Cop made a more supportive, focused relationship between churches and policing teams possible. In opening up new channels of communication, Adopt a Cop made it easier for officers to access the community through churches, as databases of local churches could be useful to home beat officers. 'If an officer wanted to access a church community, they could quickly get in touch with the pastor,' says Andy. 'Even for small things like crime prevention talks or property marking, there was a new avenue open for those home beat officers.'

God was already stirring the minds and hearts of these key Christian officers and through them and the work of the Holy Spirit in their lives, Street Pastors found a voice that could be heard. There were other senior officers, some of whom were

Christians, some of whom were not, who were open to creative solutions and were willing to try whatever tools they had at their disposal. I'm especially grateful to Sergeant Tony Unthank who helped Street Pastors get established in the borough of Lewisham; Lambeth borough commander, Chief Superintendent Dick Quinn; and Sean Wilson, then an Inspector in Brixton. Bob Pull, also an Inspector then, tells how becoming a Christian twenty years into his police career gave him 'an unquenchable desire to bring communities together and build bridges between communities and the police'. Just as I had been influenced by meeting the pastors from Pennsylvania several years earlier, and by David Shosanya's reports from Boston, Inspector Pull describes how he was struck by a newspaper article about pastors who were used as peacemakers in American cities. It had kindled a response in him, before he had ever heard anything about Street Pastors or me.

Bob was chairman for the Metropolitan Police branch of the CPA between 2000 and 2004. He saw an opportunity for service and offered himself to work with a new department, set up after the Stephen Lawrence Inquiry, which was called the Racial and Violent Crime Task Force. This new role included working as a coordinator to build bridges between black majority churches and the police in London. He knew from his experience in churches of the challenges that the black communities faced. For example, when Damilola Taylor was murdered in Peckham on 27 November 2000, there was a critical opportunity for prayer and sowing seeds of trust. Bob arranged for local church ministers to meet with the assistant pastor from the church that Damilola and his mother attended. The Met's Borough Liaison Officer in Southwark, Chief Inspector Paul Hill (a committed Christian) also attended. As a result of this meeting, on 7 April 2001, 500 Christians marched through the North Peckham Estate to pray at the spot where Damilola died and to deliver leaflets to every household, seeking information to find his murderers.

The Black Police Association led by CI Leroy Logan were supportive of the CPA's work, and together teams of black and white Christian police officers would attend black majority churches across the capital to pray with and even sing to congregations. These officers and many of their colleagues were working as 'peace officers' on the frontline of community relations.

I asked Andy Coles if the police thought that the Church could be an honest broker for a stronger relationship between the police and the community. He told me, 'No, we didn't think of it that way. We simply wanted to be open to God's leading and we knew that prayer was a powerful but neutral way to engage with the whole concept. Very few people complain about being prayed for, even police officers! Prayer is a force that you can't really stop. I'm happy to say, though, that the fallout from the prayer initiative was that communities accepted the police far more readily.'

Adopt a Cop encouraged Christians and churches to sustain prayerful support for individual officers and policing teams as they carried out their task of keeping the peace. It encouraged the Christian community to play its part in response to the Bible's command to pray for those in authority, and to show its active support for specific officers, staff teams at their local police station, and specific places and issues in their locality. The initiative is now a strand in the CPA's community engagement under the name Co-Act and has been augmented (and replaced) by Pray4YourPolice.

It seems to me that the attitude of many Christian police officers and the theme of partnership promoted by Adopt a Cop was a remarkable force for good and a path-breaker for the kind of cross-community engagement that I and the founding partners of Street Pastors were looking for. Back in 2003, church members who wanted to pray for their police teams were often the ones who were likely to support and resource Street Pastors. In addition to their unqualified support, the CPA saw Street Pastors as something that would run hand-in-hand with Adopt a Cop, with both initiatives inspiring the development of a 'whole community' response to crime and antisocial behaviour.

Pragmatic senior officers agreed to invitations to talk to me and Eustace Constance because of the Met's new alertness to grass-roots action against crime and because, if we were offering a way to cut crime rates, they were happy to hear our plans and take a view on them. At New Scotland Yard on 29 March, CI Logan and Inspector Pull opened the batting. They informed Eustace Constance and me about the expectations of the Metropolitan Police regarding risk assessments and procedures around the handing-in of weapons. The surrender of weapons was the starting point for our discussions and although, ten years later, this is not a live issue for many Street Pastors areas, it was clearly the entry point to our partnership with the Met in 2003. The two most significant issues for the police, in and around Brixton at this time (a borough that was attracting increasing amounts of political interest), were street crime and drug dealing. Though different to the contexts that the majority of street pastors work in now, back when Street Pastors was launched, it was the likelihood of a street pastor coming across a gun or a knife that made these early negotiations with the police so vital, and influenced the content of the many hours of discussion.

When we returned to New Scotland Yard for a second meeting, we were told that officers had made contact with forces around the world to enquire about their experiences involving the surrender of weapons through intermediaries. Police departments in Canada, Australia, New Zealand, South Africa and France were consulted.

This was the beginning of a long and complex but, ultimately, game-changing discussion with the Met about protocols governing the work of street pastors volunteers. Eventually we jointly produced an agreement between the police and Street Pastors and, though this was a prototype, today it is still these principles that govern the work of every volunteer and every team.

These big steps in our partnership with the police took place alongside a good deal of scrutiny about our motives and track record. At this time we were operating in two London boroughs, so we had a small body of experience to draw on and the police had something to observe and evaluate. In the first two years of operation, some quarters of the force believed that we would be a liability – that we would be out of our depth – and senior officers were keenly interested in the risks we would face and the risks we would pose. They always had more questions than we had answers. As time went by, I realised that, for the Met, this process required an extraordinary blend of innovation and scrutiny. Our discussions ranged from considerations about the surrender of weapons to a third party, to the maintenance of the independence of Street Pastors, through to general legal principles and risk management.

As representatives of Ascension Trust, Eustace and I made every effort to use the language of citizenship, rather than any Christian jargon, to make clear our identity and articulate our belief that there was a gap in police–community relations that Street Pastors could fill.

The draft agreement between the Metropolitan Police Service, Ascension Trust and the Home Office was produced in April 2004 after much rewriting and consultation. It was, in effect, a shortcut to getting the support of other boroughs in London (and cities beyond), because it made a great difference to how seriously we were taken. The agreement centred on the Metropolitan area and, although it was tailored for use in five London boroughs classed as 'hot spots', and addressed protocol for a street pastor who came across a weapon or drugs, it would also be usable in any other area that set up a Street Pastors team.

The prototype agreement represented a massive show of confidence in the Street Pastors initiative. It meant that the Met and the Home Office believed that we were doing something good, for which they wanted to create structures and policies to help us to work safely and effectively.

The protocol has stood us in good stead. This was brought home to me very clearly the night I took a call from a parent in a suburban area where we didn't have an agreement with the police. This parent had been very distressed to find a bag of drugs in his son's bedroom and wanted to talk to me urgently. I spent three hours with that man and his wife that evening. We talked about the implications of their son not being able to pay the dealer, and I advised them to find the money and give it to their son so that he could avoid the serious consequences of not paying. When I left their house I took the bag of drugs with me.

So, there I was, in an area where there was no clarifying agreement with the police, with a bag of skunk weed in my car. Before I drove off I made a call from my mobile phone to one of the officers I had been dealing with in Lambeth so that the time and location of that call was logged on my phone and his. Then, as I drove back into London, I had one of the most urgent and intimate prayer meetings I have ever had with the Lord! It was a tense drive back towards Lambeth, with me praying all the way. I let out an almighty 'hallelujah' when I crossed into the borough of Lambeth.

In 2004 the agreement was available to officers in the Met, via the Met's intranet, and any new coordinators that wished to establish a Street Pastors team could take it to meetings with police officers in other parts of the country. It wasn't a didactic document but a template that a new area could contextualise to fit their situation, and it was available to be used in each of the forty-four police authorities in England and Wales. In the space of a year, however, as we saw the initiative growing fast, with Street Pastors arriving in more and more areas, we quickly realised that a national standard agreement would be desirable. Negotiations for this national agreement began in early 2005, and officers from the Met helped us to take our document to the Association of Chief Police Officers (ACPO).

In 2007, it was used as the basis for a national protocol for other faith-based groups. This document uses broader language so that, from a police perspective, it can cover other organisations. At the time of writing, negotiations for an agreement to cover the whole of the UK are on the ACPO agenda. We are looking to get approval first from the Metropolitan Police for a redrafted Met-wide agreement, and then, when this is established, we will use it to present a document to ACPO for ratification. Though these are slow and complex processes, I believe that Ascension Trust has oiled the wheels of the debate about the police force's work with the voluntary sector and contributed to the understanding that there is such a thing as a 'civic duty' (the responsibility of all of us) as well as a statutory duty (upheld by the police) to assist in the prevention of crime and the well-being of communities. Street Pastors has been instrumental in the recognition that the battle against crime will not be won by law enforcement on its own, a principle that has caused a remarkable sea-change in policing in the UK.

Evaluation

Measuring street pastors against law enforcement criteria certainly meant, in the early days, that we looked ill-prepared or naive. Our challenge was to show the police that we could be well prepared in terms of safety, policies and procedures, and that they would need a different scale to measure us on. Would they be able to make this switch and see us as street-savvy peacemakers and inclusive befrienders? They had to acknowledge that though we might be putting ourselves in harm's way, we were doing so on different terms and with different tools in our tool box. Chief Inspector Sean Wilson, who at the time had responsibility for Brixton town centre, watched on a CCTV screen as street pastors approached a group of drug dealers and knelt down to pray with one man. 'I couldn't believe that,' he said. 'The CAD staff [Computer Aided Despatch] in the control room were all glued to the CCTV screen: they couldn't believe their eyes either.'

I was very aware in these early days of our relationship with the police how many times I wanted to say, 'We are Christians; please accept us as such.' I feel that nobody should expect us to be anything other than that, but we want everyone to understand that we are informed, socially conscious people, with a faith that challenges us to be relevant and responsible. Often we are viewed through the filters of political correctness, prejudice, the dictates of tolerance or the charge of exclusivity. But thankfully, what I have been part of is a growing will and determination among police and local government structures to work with other groups, and a realisation that the elements of this 'urban trinity' are stronger together than they are separately. In addition, all of these service providers are now working with reduced budgets and smaller numbers of staff and this, no doubt, has provided new impetus to test out the value of working with the voluntary sector.

One of the first statistical analyses of criminal behaviour in areas where street pastors were working came from Peckham, in an area that covered Rye Lane along Camberwell Church Street and into Peckham Road. Street pastors began to walk that mile regularly in 2004, and for a thirteen-week period in 2004–05, compared to the same period in 2003–04, a Southwark Council-funded report showed that serious disorder offences reduced on average by 95 per cent in the patrol area. Reductions in crime rates in other towns and cities have been reported since then. Street Pastors teams are also scrutinised as one element in partnership initiatives in which a variety of agencies and strategies – city liaison groups, neighbourhood plans, community safety plans, CCTV operations – work together for the benefit of the locality. This has meant that Street Pastors teams have, in many places, become an integrated part of the response to crime and antisocial behaviour. A 2012 presentation by the police at the Carlisle city centre group is one example of this. Street Pastors are listed among the following factors contributing to a 45 per cent drop in violent crime in the city:

Dispersal orders

Designated Public Place orders.

Street closure: Botchergate, the main area of bars and clubs is gated on Saturday night/Sunday morning. Police can circulate with the public and 'meet and greet'.

Best Bar None competition: An annual event to pick the best bars in town . . . bars can get advice on how to be more user-friendly.

Test purchases scheme: Under police supervision, underage teenagers try to buy alcohol in bars. Those bars caught selling to them are dealt with and the message spreads throughout the industry.

Street Pastors: Their work is described as 'phenomenal' by police officers.

Taxi-rank marshals: Specially trained door staff patrol the taxi ranks to enable orderly journeys home.

Passive drugs dogs: Sweeps are done and drugs are found.

Pub Watch scheme: Has eighty members in Carlisle. Public who get banned from a pub/bar can face a three-year ban.

CCTV – Two types: (a) public as part of the Pub Watch scheme and (b) a deployable police CCTV van, parked in busy areas. CCTV on taxi rank, too.

Though we must always make it clear that we are independent of the police, Street Pastors teams are now considered by many forces to be part of the wider policing family. Over time more figures and statistics have been generated around and for the work of Street Pastors teams, and this has started to include ways of expressing the benefits of Street Pastors in terms of what their work saves the public purse. A recent press release from Devon and Cornwall CPA makes this kind of calculation when it notes that 'a total of 849 hours of patrol time were being provided across the two counties every week by street pastors and school pastors. This equates to 44,148 hours over the course of 2012. This figure does not include time given up for training or in administration.'

It is acknowledged that if each pastor was paid the national minimum wage (£6.19 per hour) this represents a financial contribution in 2012 to the policing of the evening and night-time economy (ENTE) and school premises in Devon and Cornwall of £273,276.12. The press release ends by scaling up these figures by using the living wage rate of £7.45, which would see the figure rise to £328,902.60 (and that does not take into account any antisocial shift allowance normally provided for those working at night).

Likewise, a 'Safe Place' scheme in Falmouth, Cornwall, which is an extension of the work of the Street Pastors team in the town, was declared to have saved the public purse £1,700 in three months, according to the *West Briton* newspaper (21 February 2013). Whether it comes from a statistical, socio-logical or budgetary point of view, evaluation is something that we welcome. It might be undertaken by external bodies (for example, universities or public health groups), by police forces or by Street Pastors coordinators themselves, part of whose job it is to find ways of 'showing and telling' the nature of the engagement they have with people.

@DC_CPA

Based on yesterdays #StreetPastors conference in last 12m, given 44,148 hours patrolling worth £27,3276.12 if paid min wage! #devon

Making good use of street pastors

Increasingly street pastors are being valued as a 'good fit' with the aims of the police and other statutory and non-statutory groups whose focus is on making their town or city a welcoming place to visit both during the daytime and at night. This means that street pastors are becoming involved in projects that extend their work, either in terms of days/hours on patrol or in terms of initiatives that they can help to operate. For example, in Aberdeen (and several other places around the country), a Safe Space bus, launched with the support of a variety of partners, including Grampian Police, provides care and support in the city centre and supplements the work already carried out by Street Pastors volunteers.

In Reading, Newcastle, and elsewhere, police have encouraged door staff to work with street pastors through Door Watch schemes. Through initiatives like this, licensees, door supervisors and the police work together to improve safety for customers and reduce crime and disorder. Door staff are often responsive to working with street pastors in this way and, together, they are able to make sure that when someone is ejected from a club or pub, street pastors are on hand to make sure they get home or find their friends safely. These examples show how the Street Pastors' teams are being deployed to strengthen the public safety net.

The police are also often actively involved in the training of new volunteers. A safety officer may outline strategies for managing conflict, or a CCTV operator will make sure that recruits are trained in using the radios so that they can be fully linked to the CCTV system.

@shrewsburySP
Hereford City to have Street Pastors patrolling streets in May. 15 volunteers already signed up – and another 10 or so tonight.#godisgood!

Hard facts and soft skills

Our partnership with the police has developed so much that Ascension Trust receives enquiries about setting up a new Street Pastors area or team more often from a police officer than from a church leader. One such example of the police initiating the set-up of a new team was reported recently in Spalding in Lincolnshire. After interest among local councillors in establishing a Street Pastors team in the town, the community policing inspector, Inspector Jim Tyner, called on church members in the area to back plans for the scheme in an interview with the local paper, the *Spalding Guardian* on 16 February 2013. The inspector said, 'Lincolnshire Police and South Holland District Council have been working closely with Churches Together in Spalding and District to see how we could introduce Street Pastors in the town, as it has been very well received in other communities across the county'. Four days later, the paper reported that thirty people had attended an information evening and a presentation by Sergeant Stuart Hurst. After the meeting, Sergeant Hurst said that he was involved in the plans 'because the police in Spalding think that any group of people who are keen to show an interest and support the vulnerable in our community is extremely welcome' (20 February 2013).

Why do police officers want to find ways of working with street pastors? The police know that there is great strength in the voluntary sector and volunteers in general. DCC Rob Beckley, police service lead for Citizens in Policing, comments that volunteers 'are not bound by the preconceived notions that accompany a police uniform. Volunteer groups can speak to people who will not speak to the police, they can correct misconceptions about what the police are about and how we operate, they can build bridges into communities. We are there to work with people and groups in communities to assist in making and keeping areas safe. This demands partnerships in all areas of society.'

Street Pastors are independent of the police, but they can provide an additional layer of support to local policing. This is probably best seen in the way that a street pastor has time to engage with an individual, whereas an officer has to cope with many calls on his or her time. Police officers are working hard to understand and find ways of engaging with troubled areas and troubled families, but it can take them a long time given all the other demands they have to juggle.

One of the liberating things about leaving home in the middle of the evening and staying out on the streets into the small hours is that you leave the computer, the emails and the phone calls behind. Though a street pastor is part of busy, noisy, often unpalatable street scenes, which can often be demanding and draining, they are people who have made themselves available and are there to give time to other people. They go out ready to focus on another person. They are people who have the ability to give time generously and lovingly; they are people who have the potential to soak up aggression. When they go out with their team they are seeking to understand others, not condemn them.

Over the ten years since 2003 there has been a growing appreciation of the 'soft' skills that a street pastor can bring. As I've already described, at the outset, many police officers thought our pastoral, 'shepherding' skills would be out of place in the night-time economy, making us a liability to ourselves and others. They were seeing street pastors dealing with some of the same difficult people and doing some tasks that were similar to those an officer would carry out, but they were *without* body armour or the other pieces of kit that an officer has. As time has gone by, however, and our credibility has grown, it has brought some understanding of what exactly is in our 'tool kit' and how our people skills can actually be put to good use on the front line of a dispute or when drunken aggression builds up or when emotional turmoil is released. Police officers connect with individuals in a very short moment of time, whereas street pastors can focus on needy individuals so that officers can use their time more efficiently.

Take, for example, the following scenario. A police officer comes across a man in his mid-forties who is drunk and not able to stand up. Police protocol says that the officer should call an ambulance to get the man checked over. Protocol also dictates that someone who is drunk and incapable in a public place should be arrested. So, besides the paramedics and the ambulance, two more officers will be tied up with this man, who will need to be taken into custody after he has been examined by the medics. One last option for the officer is to stay with the man for a while to see if he sobers up. All these possible courses of action involve the time and resources of several people and services. The officer that outlined this scenario to me then went on to say that what actually happened in this particular case was that a street pastor made himself known to the officer and asked if there was anything he could do. The officer asked if the street pastor could stay with the man, making clear that he would return as soon as he could. The street pastor waited with the man, covered him in a silver foil blanket and checked that when he vomited he was not endangering himself further. When the officer returned, the man had sobered up slightly and was no longer in need of an ambulance. From an operational point of view, the street pastor saved the police a tremendous amount of time and resources.

Relations between a Street Pastors team and a policing team: What is good practice?

Stability

Street pastors are looking for stability in the policing teams they work with. Inevitably, when there are budget cuts, forces have to cope with restructuring and change. In many cities and towns, neighbourhood teams have got smaller and may have to cover a wider area. In Newquay in Cornwall, however, street pastors were able to work effectively during the peak summer months of 2012, because they say that they were operating alongside a dedicated police team attached to the area for the summer period.

Standard Operating Practices (SOP) agreement

The SOP agreement helps forge good relations between street pastors and police teams, and is important in overcoming any misunderstanding about the street pastors' role or hostility from officers towards volunteers. When practices and expectations are set out clearly, the tone is set for better professional understanding of each other's role and for stating the motivation for the role of a street pastor. The SOP, a direct descendant of the protocol agreement between the Metropolitan Police and Ascension Trust, made in 2004, is also useful as a way of starting conversations between local officers and volunteers when a new Street Pastors area is at the planning stages. It may sometimes be known as a Memorandum of Understanding (MOU). Professional standards for street pastors are increasingly vital in contexts where a number of bodies and partners are involved in delivering neighbourhood safety initiatives.

Briefings and distribution lists

It is good practice for one member of the Street Pastors team to be present at the police briefing on the night of a patrol, or vice versa, for an officer on duty to come along to the Street Pastors' team briefing. Sometimes this is difficult for the officer, who may be called away at the last minute. Some teams use CCTV as point of contact between the police and them; CCTV operators can tell them what to expect on a particular night, whether any missing persons have been reported, etc. All Street Pastors teams should have a dedicated police telephone number for the duration of their patrol.

Street Pastors teams compile distribution lists. These are usually weekly reports containing the numbers of volunteers on patrol and any particular descriptions of activity or incident from the weekend's patrols. Sending these reports to the policing team is a good way to build a relationship with officers on duty and a useful way of emphasising professionalism.

Regular meetings between street pastors and police inspector

Developing a relationship with a local police inspector is always beneficial. In addition, neighbourhood teams generally have quarterly meetings, and street pastors' coordinators could be part of that. An opportunity for open discussion, a place you can air difficulties and break down suspicions or concerns about the role of a street pastor, is always a good thing.

Sergeant Gary Watts first became aware of Street Pastors when he was working in a project development role and realised they were pestering his assistant chief constable for a share of a pot of money he was also interested in. He describes how his antagonism turned into admiration as some months later he began to work with Street Pastors in Falmouth.

I didn't see why the police should give money to Street Pastors. So the first impression that I formed was that Street Pastors was another case of Christians pushing themselves forward to get something for themselves.

A year later I was posted back from headquarters in Exeter to frontline service in Falmouth. Here I came across more Christians; this time they were officers in my neighbourhood team. One of these officers was on the management committee of the local Street Pastors team. I was asked to join him on the committee and I agreed, although I was sceptical about what they did. In truth, I thought it would put me in a good position to put a stop to anything I thought was improper. I thought they would be preaching, and didn't want that to have anything to do with policing.

I met the management team; they were nice people. It didn't seem like they would have anything to do with preaching. The first thing I noticed was that their motives were my motives: we both wanted to care for the people of Falmouth and make sure that they were safe. Though we would have a different role – they wouldn't jump in to prevent a fight like a police officer – they would be on the scene, too, and with the same motives. So I started monitoring them, engaging with them and working with the management committee. I soon began to realise that there wasn't any preaching involved in what they did.

I discovered that a link between the police and street pastors would be beneficial. They would do a lot of the same things as I would do on a Friday or Saturday night – looking after people who hadn't committed a crime but had got into a state and weren't able to look after themselves. Before street pastors were around we would have had to do that alone. So it was obvious that one benefit of street pastors is that they can release a police officer to do other parts of their job. I would say that now I'm a big advocate of what they do and I take any opportunity I can to change any negative opinions at the station. The street pastors themselves often find that I'm pestering them to work on other nights besides a Saturday!

In fact, in Falmouth – a university town with a high proportion of under-twenty-five-year-olds – we have taken our relationship with Street Pastors a step further. At the end of 2012 we developed an independent project that street pastors helped to set up along with other agencies. It's called the Safe Space project, and it runs parallel to the street pastors' normal activities and ours. It's not a faith-driven project at all, and it's run by volunteers from the local community. It complements the rest of what we try to do because if officers or street pastors come across anyone in need or incapable they get taken to the Safe Space. It frees both of us up.

Whereas in the past, street pastors might have had to spend up to an hour with someone out in the cold, waiting for that person to be able to communicate their name, or find a friend or family member who can take them home, now they can arrange for that person to be taken back to Safe Space. It's not a café, we keep the doors locked, but once someone has been taken there, the volunteers can then make a decision about what to do and the street pastors can get back on the street, because that's where they are most useful. I know of one student who joined Safe Space because of his contact with street pastors. He was out in the town one night, drunk, got himself into a vulnerable position because he couldn't look after himself, and street pastors took care of him. That's why he joined Safe Space as a volunteer.

In my experience the university students especially take to the street pastors. On nights when they are not operating, we get people running up to us, asking us where they are. They're good at standing around having a chat.

Yes, street pastors have different tools to police officers. They *have such an 'easy-in' because they are not the police. There's no barrier between them and the public, like there is between us and the public. So often heavy-handed policing skills are not what is needed; the ability to talk to people is more valuable.*

FAQ

In England and Wales the Police have nearly 20,000 Special Constables, 10,000 Police Support volunteers, 4 million neighbourhood watch members and 10,000 street pastors. Has the police's interest in working alongside voluntary groups gone too far?

These figures equate to 30,000 directed and controlled volunteers within the police service. When you put this into the context of the 200,000 people working within the police service it is a healthy, not excessive, figure. The police service was founded on a number of principles that Sir Robert Peel considered to be the bedrock on which the modern police service should operate. Often the most recited of these principles sets the scene for an answer to this question:

Police, at all times, should maintain a relationship with the public that gives reality to the historic tradition that the police are the public and the public are the police; the police being only members of the public who are paid to give full-time attention to duties which are incumbent upon every citizen in the interests of community welfare and existence.

So in fact our interest lies in working alongside over sixty-two million people! This is not about direction and control,

---

this is about operating in a society where policing is not separate from society, but part of it. It is about society being confident that people will look after each other and will work with policing to ensure, wherever possible, that the police are not required. There are improvements to be made in how we shape our relationships with the voluntary sector, but one must always remember *'the police are the public and the public are the police'*: it is our duty to society to work together wherever and in as many ways as possible to ensure a safer, cohesive society.

Rob, Chief Operating Officer for the College of Policing

7

Towards a strong and informed voluntary sector:
Street Pastors and statutory partners

When I wrote about Ascension Trust's early relationships with the public sector in my first book about our work (*Street Pastors*, Kingsway, 2009), the opening paragraph contained the words 'patchy' and 'variable'. The second paragraph added 'tense', 'suspicious' and 'cold'. In picking this story up here, four years after the first book and ten years after the birth of Street Pastors, I can paint a different picture. I believe that the outlook has changed and that, more often than not, scepticism has given way to acceptance in most relationships between a Street Pastors team and its partners in local government. Street Pastors is now one of several nationwide projects that are capturing the attention of central and local government, food banks and CAP (Christians Against Poverty) being two other examples. An important debate has recently been brought to the House of Commons, triggered by a report produced by Christians in Parliament and the Evangelical Alliance, entitled 'Faith in the Community', which discusses cooperation between faith groups and public services. The debate credits faith-led voluntary or charitable groups with a great range of compassionate services, from language classes to bereavement counselling to toddler groups, and refers to the valued and vital partnerships between local authorities and faith groups

7
115

working for the benefit of communities. This chapter looks, from the point of view of Street Pastors, at the journey so far in the cooperation between public services and national and local faith-led groups.

From hearing the experiences of management teams and coordinators up and down the country, I know that although the broad picture of relationships between areas covered by Street Pastors and city and town councils is more favourable now than it was when the initiative started, there is still a broad spectrum of relationships. Some areas are taking small steps in their partnerships, others are able to take longer strides. Some teams have been able to take the foundation of coopera-tion that Street Pastors has forged and deepen and extend what they can do alongside the public sector. Others are finding that warming up the relationship is a long-term process and that practical (aside from financial) support for their role takes a long time to materialise. In one coastal resort, the Street Pastors coordinator asked the council for public toilets to be opened on a Friday and Saturday night during their patrol time. After four years of discussions and an eventual agreement about different working practices for the toilet cleaners, street pastors now open the public toilets at the start of their shift and lock them up again before they go home. Local authority funding varies greatly, too. Some areas have received significant sums of money, whereas in other places, councils say that they would never be able to support one faith group to the same extent.

Innovation and support takes many forms, however, and whether it's the provision of free parking for volunteers when they are on duty, or council agencies who ask to join street pastors on patrol to see what they can learn about their priority areas, all Street Pastors areas have made progress in terms of support from – or establishing credibility with – local authori-ties. Staying faithful to their role and responsibilities under scrutiny, and clearly articulating who they are and what they do, has helped many teams deepen their formal and informal statutory partnerships. Suspicion and antagonism towards Street Pastors from local authorities does still exist, but my fervent hope is that councils will put the greater good of the community first. For our part we must do whatever we can to reassure councils that we are genuine in our conviction and care for the lives of other people.

@WhitingtonSteve
Listening to 3 girls talking about @StreetPastors on the train – they appreciate these terrific bunch of street guardians

It's very typical that the starting point for this journey is uncertainty. This was certainly the case for Ascension Trust as we tried to engage the interest and support of local government – the third arm of the 'urban trinity' – in 2003. At that time, after the fruitfulness of our relationships with Operation Trident, the Metropolitan branch of the Christian Police Association and the senior officers in the Met who wrestled with the draft agreement for the operational side to the work of Street Pastors, I assumed Ascension Trust would receive a warm welcome from the London boroughs that we approached. In fact we found that professional judgement was often clouded by individual prejudices, and we had to work hard even to get a toe in the door. This is less evident now that we have a track record to draw on, but a more recent example of the strength of secularism in some local government offices is shown by one city council, which said that Christians caring for other people was 'patronising'. In 2003 we managed to get just one council official to attend the launch evening in Brixton Baptist Church.

When a council is uncertain about supporting Street Pastors, they are saying that they are 'not sure' what we are about, 'not sure' whether we will do what we say we will do, or whether we will, in fact, turn out to be hardline evangelicals. They are concerned that if they endorse us, they might be endorsing the Church to preach at people. Ten years ago, I felt that polarisation between many churches and local authorities meant that a lot of councils were out of touch with what local churches were doing in their communities. In addition, when they looked at me they saw a black man – a black man who was a minister of the church – and straightaway they assumed I would be preaching and telling everyone they were sinners. Instead of hearing what I was saying about today's challenges, councillors and officials were recalling past tensions between the Church and government. Many of the councils that we wanted to work with were not sure they wanted to be seen to support us. In some cases we were told that they did not want to fund an exclusively Christian organisation.

Happily, our journey did not end there, and where Street Pastors teams have also encountered uncertainty over the ten years since then, it has generally not stopped councils from watching and waiting to see what they deliver. I'm not aware of any council that has withdrawn its support or kept its distance from a Street Pastors team over the long term. Ascension Trust always encourages coordinators to take six months to a year to consult, to look at other schemes in their region and, above all, to talk to their local council. This allows all parties the chance to develop friendships and to gather information. It is essential that a team has the support of the local police and, with this in place, we often find that the message about working with Street Pastors filters through to the council, either because good news travels or because councillors are asking direct questions of the police about their evaluation of us.

In the months that followed the launch of Street Pastors in 2003, in parallel to developing a working relationship with the police, we began to explore ways we could work with the boroughs that we had visited during the 'Guns on our streets' tour. In terms of actual night-time patrols, Lambeth was the first borough where Street Pastors began to operate on the streets, Hackney was the second, and Lewisham was the third. In Lambeth and Hackney we just had to get on with operations on our own, with our own finances, but with the borough of Lewisham our efforts for support and partnership came to life and, by being part of the community safety team, we were able to be part of the council's discussions about the problems the borough was facing. Immediately we were playing a different ball game. The council was saying that it believed in us, we were involved in a more formal partnership, and they were observing our negotiations on the protocol agreement with the Metropolitan Police.

Lewisham Council was aware of problems with guns and gangs in neighbouring boroughs and was alert to the way in which these could easily become a problem in Lewisham itself. I was impressed with the councillors I met; they weren't in denial but were acknowledging that prevention is better than cure. With us they were truly moving by faith, making space for innovation and saying, 'Let's see if Street Pastors can help.' For the small team at Ascension Trust, it felt like the penny had at last dropped.

After volunteering to be part of the first batch of trainees, Eustace Constance became the first Street Pastors coordinator for the borough of Lewisham, a two-year post made possible by a sum of money from Lewisham Council. The first few months in Lewisham required an extraordinary level of work from Eustace and a commitment to talk to as many of the civic and administrative key players in the borough as possible, from the lord mayor through to housing officers. In return the council kept its ear to the ground and received information from the police and local people. Through this, together with our weekly reports, they evaluated the work we were doing.

For many Street Pastors teams all over the country, early

relationships have required a lot of effort and a determination to communicate the message that 'we would rather do this with you than without you'. The benefits of a hard-won relationship with a statutory partner, however, are often considerable; as they keep travelling together, Street Pastors teams talk about reaching 'turning points' and 'landmarks', about the growth of trust and the establishment of credibility that happens when remits are extended and areas of commonality are grasped. The analysis of Street Pastors and statutory partners in this chapter will take you on some of the journeys travelled by teams around the UK and outline a picture of growing integration and agreement between Street Pastors and the public sector.

Why work with statutory partners?

I knew when I read Raymond Bakke's book *The Urban Christian* (1987), and came across the term 'urban trinity', that Street Pastors teams had to be in partnership with town and city councils for three main reasons: first, to make the principle of collaboration central; second, to give us credibility; and third, so that our volunteers can effectively signpost people to the services they need. We need to understand what the local authority is doing, how they shape the place that we live in and the lives that we lead, how public services work and how they can be accessed. They, on the other hand, need to be comfortable with us and understand what we do. We need to complement each other in the belief that when people and groups come together, they can make a positive change. When groups and services do their own thing, I would argue, and independence becomes a primary aim, the indicators show that people fall through the gaps between services.

In terms of credibility, working with the backing of local government means that Street Pastors teams are officially recognised, with a structure for accountability. One street pastor tells how during one patrol, a resident came out of a nearby house, asking who they were and why were they hanging around young people. Answering an enquiry like this is a lot easier if you can say that you are backed by the council and the police.

On the other hand, street pastors need to make it clear that they are not affiliated to either the police or the local council. Where Street Pastors teams work in housing estates and residential areas, they have sometimes come across the assumption that they will take on the same role as the community 'bobby on the beat' might once have done, as, with the decline in community policing, many members of the public would like to see more 'official' people on the streets. Where there are groups of young people hanging around, who might expect to be moved on or dispersed by the police, street pastors will, however, simply chat about what they are doing, wish them a good night, and walk away. It is important that they know that street pastors are not policing them in any way.

Approached by an onlooker during a patrol one night, a Street Pastors volunteer told me how they listened to this person's angry verbal assault about the problem of homelessness in their town. That onlooker thought they were making an official complaint to a housing official. When the street pastor told the man that all members of the team were volunteers from local churches, his anger was diffused. I'm not trying to say that street pastors can switch colours pragmatically, and distance themselves from or align themselves with statutory partners as suits the moment, but my point is that both elements of our identity, the impartial and the integrated, are important. Sometimes we have to help people with their perception of our role.

@halfon4harlowMP
After starting at 2200, I now say good bye to #Harlow #StreetPastors. They do another patrol around town until 4am

Signposting

A referral takes places when a street pastor is able to directly introduce one person to another, or one person to a service. Signposting is a more informal kind of introduction; it might mean giving out the phone number of a service or an agency, or discussing with someone whether they are aware of such-and-such a service. Many people are not good at accessing the services they need, or they find the system too intimidating, or require a level of order and organisation that does not exist in their lives. The angry onlooker described above shows us that some people are in need of a tangible, human point of contact, a face in a system that can be too faceless. As they go out to people and meet people on their own turf, street pastors find that, in some cases, they are acting as a bridge between the individual and the service provider.

A significant milestone for us was the publication in December 2004 of a double-page article in the local government newspaper, *Lambeth Life*. The positive report was accompanied by a logo depicting the 'urban trinity', in this case, the borough of Lambeth/Metropolitan Police/Church, and a caption that read, 'The local authority provides education and social services. The police maintain law and order. The Church has a spiritual, caring role. Each one has responsibility for the welfare of the community.' The transition from scepticism to welcome was still ongoing in Lambeth and in many other city halls and departments, but *Lambeth Life*, remarkably, set out our relevance to local authorities very clearly. It announced that Street Pastors would 'act as a buffer, a bridge and intermediary or referral service for people who need it . . . '

A street pastor's ability to signpost someone to the service they need depends in large part on the relationship between their team and local statutory providers. The more developed the team's relationship with housing services departments, emergency shelters, environmental health officers or job clubs, the better they are able to refer people to those services. Trust and professionalism in partnerships between the voluntary sector and the statutory sector therefore have a direct bearing on the effectiveness of signposting.

Street pastors in Taunton tell how at 2 a.m. one night they were taking a break between patrols at the rest room at their base, when there was an urgent banging on the door. On the doorstep they found a distressed couple from a central Mediterranean country, saying 'We must talk to street pastors.' The volunteers listened to a heartbreaking story of the abortion the woman had undergone a week earlier, and the guilt she was feeling, compounded by the fact that nothing had been spoken about it between the couple until then. The street pastors were able to put the couple in touch with a counselling service operated by local Christians. Many street pastors find that they meet members of the armed services, who are out in the pubs and clubs to forget what they have experienced on tour; many are anxious for street pastors to pray with them. This is particularly evident in Taunton, the nearest town to the 40 Commando Royal Marines. Street pastors in Taunton are able to put serving and former military personnel in touch with the provider of a free, eight-week outreach programme addressing post-traumatic stress disorder (PTSD), offered by the charity PTSD Resolution. That is a tremendous asset to their relationships with the Royal Marines and a timely referral at the point at which a person is ready to engage with their distress and talk about it.

@stevetierney
I'd love to see street pastors here. I think they're wonderful.

Starting up

Mark Hadfield, coordinator of Street Pastors in Inverness, says that the relationship with their statutory partners was brought to life as the city council began to look for answers to the most basic of questions: what can we see of value in these street pastors? Signposting was one of the answers that they could identify, but the council still had plenty of doubts. 'In the end, they were willing to try us out,' says Mark. Five-and-a-half years ago when Street Pastors in Inverness was launched, councillors and reporters from the local press were invited to come out with the team and observe them in action. The Street Pastors team was clear that they must stay faithful to their training and simply let people see what they did. As Mark adds:

Street Pastors was a partner in a city centre group, made up of agencies working in drug and alcohol recovery, together with several city councillors. Early on in our work I was at one of these particular meetings, and the agencies represented were sharing news and views, and I was pretty quiet as I didn't have much to share. I thought things were drawing to a close when the provost said, 'We have a few minutes left, so I'd like to say something about the Street Pastors.' I held my breath. 'We've had lots of discussions about you, and we've been very sceptical, but we were wrong. You are an essential part of this partnership.' This gave us so much confidence and discussions with all of our partners in the town and in the council changed from that point on.

A shared understanding and trusting partnership was in place right from the start in Southampton in 2009, where the scheme was seen as a wonderful 'joining up' around shared goals. Prior to this time, the city's main night-time entertainment areas had been identified by the Home Office as far above average for violent crime and assault. Police and council heard about street pastors in neighbouring Portsmouth as they were putting together a set of measures to address the problems. Senior police officers and council officials visited the team in Portsmouth and any doubts about objectives or motivation were cleared away – there was unanimous demand for a team in Southampton. The city safety officer and the police were delighted to find that members of the church community in the city were already in touch with Ascension Trust in preparation. The partnership here was realised in a practical way – the police and city council both made senior staff available to join the management committee, they helped us find start-up funding from the Home Office and the mayor made Street Pastors one of his mayoral charities.

In Sutton, southwest London, church leader and Street Pastors coordinator Mark Tomlinson was already part of a local strategic partnership, sitting alongside chief executives and heads of the Primary Care Trust. At one meeting, one of the agencies in the Safer Sutton Partnership gave a presentation on fear of crime in the borough. Around the same time, I visited Mark's church and spoke about Street Pastors and Mark realised that the Street Pastors initiative could be one response to what he was hearing from local leaders about the fear of crime. When he started discussions with the borough council, concerns were raised about street pastors' safety. The council believed that members might have to 'spend more time watching our backs than actually achieving anything'. Within six months, however, they had agreed to make some funding available to Street Pastors in Sutton. In Sutton, as elsewhere, trust, credibility and the belief that the Street Pastors team would not overstep its remit had to be established for the partnership to strengthen. Practical demonstration was vital in Southampton, too, particularly at ground level, where door staff and police officers were scrutinising Street Pastors at an operational level.

As with other teams, Street Pastors in Liverpool echo the view that 'the proof of the pudding is in the eating'. They recount how in their city, one police officer and one council representative had faith in them at the beginning, but many others didn't. 'It was not until they saw us out on the streets that the police and the council really understood. You haven't got to tell them you're good. If you are out there every weekend, in the rain and the snow, they will see it.'

Liverpool Street Pastors is now very well received by city officials and has quickly gathered a high-profile position in the partnership between the public sector and voluntary groups. In 2010, when Liverpool was one of three areas to be awarded 'Purple Flag' status in recognition of improvements in its after-dark economy, Street Pastors was considered to be part of the turnaround. Tackling the antisocial behaviour that stops many people from enjoying a safe night out in the city has been crucial to the Kitemark award for Liverpool, and Street Pastors is mentioned as part of successful bids for the award in several other UK cities. The fact that accreditation was achieved through a variety of local partners working together was an approach that, in itself, was encouraged and recognised by Purple Flag.

Once the ball started rolling for Street Pastors in Liverpool, there were letters from grateful parents in local papers, university students following the team as part of their coursework, and interested newspaper reporters accompanying patrols on a regular basis. There was plenty of evidence to help the city council towards a favourable relationship with Street Pastors. The advice from Liverpool is simple. 'Get set up, work out where your "patch" will be, get the support of the police, and get started. Your relationship with the council will grow from that.'

What makes a good relationship between Street Pastors and the local authority?

- A Street Pastors team needs to work at understanding what their council is looking for. Listen to what they are saying. It's not a question of tailoring what you can offer in order to fill a need, but about finding areas of commonality. You may well have different views, but there will be lots of areas you can agree on;

- Be embedded in ongoing discussions in the local statutory scene – task force groups, strategy groups, safer community partnerships – before starting Street Pastors. Building good relationships in those places is key;

- Keep demonstrating what you do when you're out on patrol and invite councillors to join you as observers. This will be important for funding and support. Write reports, gather statistics, document each patrol (how many needles/glass bottles collected; what kinds of conversations you had; first aid administered, etc.). Make it possible for your work to be assessed. Continue to build your relationship with other stake-holders in city centre safety – for example, licensees and door-staff;

- Communicate the core values of Street Pastors, always being open about them. Local authorities need to understand how we engage with people, how we help people to become more aware about the environment they live in and the affect that they have on one another. Street pastors do not just divert, distract and react. What we are really concerned with is how to get to know people. Do we sincerely understand how a

person has ended up in this situation? With someone who wants to move on, how do we help them? The five core values listed in Chapter 4 are really wise and presented in a helpful way. Stick close to them; they are great things to talk about with partners;
- Be honest. Don't promise something that you can't deliver.

Austerity and the Christian-led voluntary sector

The financial crisis that we have seen across Europe and in the UK is forcing central and local governments to do things differently, with an underlying focus on prevention and demand management. Raising levels of civic engagement is a vital way to strengthen the local community and, in the context of reduced budgets for social care, it is delivering cost savings and many other benefits for existing services. Local authorities are beginning to see that they must make use of existing community assets, and through them enable lower levels of support to be more widely available. Churches and Christians represent existing community assets.

The debate about how much the state should take responsibility for the welfare and the protection of its citizens will, however, only get noisier, with the uncertainties about the changes that government deficits will bring and the restructuring of social care. The Church needs to engage in a responsible way with these financial changes, and sometimes it will find itself, as Matt Bird of the Cinnamon Network warns, holding in tension its 'responsibility to both care for the poor and challenge government policy'. Our commitment to the values of the gospel of Jesus Christ means that we want to make God visible through the practical demonstration of our faith. We won't ignore the invitation to be part of new civic structures and ways of delivering what communities need. For the Christian-led voluntary sector, the economic cuts have opened wider the door to participation in public life, enabling the Church to rediscover its calling to be the 'light of the world' and the 'salt of the earth' (Matthew 5:13–14). We must be accountable to God for the way we use this opportunity.

It's not always the case that weaker local authority provision makes room for a vibrant voluntary sector. In some cities, when it comes to the crunch, the Third Sector has been found to be depleted. This is sometimes because local government has, in better times, put all its eggs in one basket and strengthened and 'professionalised' one group at the expense of others. What is common to all of our towns and cities is that we will all be living with much greater uncertainty about how welfare reforms will impact people. Our responsibility is to make clear our identity and our role, protect our Christian ethos, and find the common ground where we can add something to state provision. Using the simplicity of our strapline 'Caring, listening and helping' as a guide, we could argue that one individual showing compassion to another, face to face, cannot be the work of the state. As Chapter 6 in particular shows, the 'soft skills' focus of street pastors complements the sharp-end work of the police, an example of the way that a faith group can add value to the work of the public services.

Innovation

Mark Hadfield, coordinator for Inverness Street Pastors, describes how the city council and Street Pastors found a 'common objective to work for peace' that led to an extension of the remit for the work of Street Pastors in the city.

Inverness's status as the prime tourist destination in the Highlands meant that the city had an image to protect – one that was not best served by alcohol-related disturbances at night. As Mark comments, 'It's a big shock for tourists from outside the UK when they come to a place with a binge-drinking culture.'

Two-and-a-half years ago we were invited to a meeting of the community safety partnership which, at the time, we weren't officially part of. It was made up of representatives from local businesses, the NHS, the ambulance service and the city council. It transpired that they had been discussing the idea of 'city ambassadors' for some time, without making progress. Like many places, trade and tourism are the drivers behind a lot of policy decisions, and the safety partnership had been talking about how Inverness city centre needs to be a welcoming place. Most people visiting the Highlands will come to Inverness, and the image of the city that tourists receive comes from their impression of its architecture and streetscape right through to their impression of the behaviour of its residents on the streets and in public places.

The council was concerned about the perception of the city and wanted to designate a group of people who could be out in the city centre during the daytime, to help guide tourists and answer people's questions. The discussion had got stuck because they didn't know who to mobilise to do this. In addition, they were starting to realise that this role was a pastoral one. So they asked us. That's how daytime Street Pastors came about in Inverness.

The journey for Inverness Street Pastors has brought them through scepticism to understanding and approval and, more recently, has moved to the council thinking of them as people who can represent city interests. The team has also found that their daytime role has involved them in helping different parts of the community relate better to each other.

Mark Hadfield describes how the divergent interests of the business community and houses of multiple occupancy/emergency shelters were causing friction in Inverness city centre. For the daytime Street Pastors team, this created an opportunity to get to know both local traders and homeless people. Understanding both groups better has meant that street pastors can represent one group to the other. Where interest groups tend to polarise, Mark sees street pastors as impartial and able to help everyone be better informed. Mark cites an example of a needle-exchange programme operating among the emergency accommodation clients. 'Staff would meet clients and collect needles. The clients themselves would also go out once a day and scour for needles,' says Mark. 'Nobody at the safety partnership meeting knew this was going on to help protect the wider community.'

More than one view needs to be represented in any city centre, and a group like Street Pastors is ideally placed to listen to all sides and bring another perspective to meetings between statutory groups and city centre stakeholders. By the same token, street pastors often find that they have a voice in council chambers and among those with city interests, *as well as* in places that are less accessible, among the homeless community or those in rehabilitation.

An independent voice contributes to the effectiveness of a Street Pastors team on and off the street. In Liverpool, the head of the city centre team comes to team meetings and asks what they think about certain things. Street pastors are able to feed back their views, such as the need for more taxis, or the relocation of a taxi rank to a different place. If the council's office staff generally finish work at 5 p.m., they may need to rely on reports about night-time activities from the police, and street pastors can add another perspective to this description. In addition, when the coordinator of Street Pastors in Liverpool goes to meetings with heads of council departments, retail bosses and the city centre team manager, he finds that because he is the only one who is a volunteer, what he has to say is respected. 'Being a street pastor is not my paid job or my career, so the effect of me being in these meetings and being out on the street at night is very positive. We find that the council really wants to hear our opinion.'

There are many ways in which Street Pastors teams are now finding that initiatives, services or facilities are being put in place by other public sector partners that add capacity to what street pastors do. The so-called 'Safe Bus' or 'Safe Space' vehicles that operate in some cities, supplement the work of street pastors and give them a mobile platform from which to work and provide a haven for those in need. An alcohol treatment centre in Cardiff, funded by the Welsh National Assembly, is another such example. The centre operates in a converted room in a local church, and has been developed through partnerships in Cardiff, of which Street Pastors is a part. Whereas in the past street pastors might have had to stay with someone incapacitated by alcohol or drugs for an hour or more, now they can call the mobile unit to come and collect that person.

Gary Smith, director of Street Pastors in Cardiff, says that street pastors refer, on average, two people to the centre each night that they are on patrol. The unit is manned by nurse practitioners from A&E and, with ten beds, it receives anyone particularly affected by alcohol or drugs, or with a minor injury. Individuals can be assessed, or left to sleep before being re-assessed, sent to A&E, or sent home.

Since its official launch in 2011, School Pastors has become a significant way in which the ethos of Street Pastors is being extended. In Southampton, when the council asked how Street Pastors could help them find solutions to other problems, the resources inherent in the team were utilised through daytime patrols as School Pastors. In Chapter 10 you can read more about how School Pastors have become the catalyst for impact and influence that is spreading out from the city to the suburbs.

As the elected mayor of the London borough of Lewisham, Sir Steve Bullock has championed the work of Street Pastors in south London. Sir Steve describes why he maintains links with a variety of voluntary organisations and what surprises him about Street Pastors.

A normal day sees me moving between emails, phone calls, meet ings with council officials, often followed by more meetings in the evening. There is always a flood of information coming in through the day; I don't need to deal with it all personally but I need to know about it. Currently Lewisham Council is working through a cuts exercise, but big challenges like London's housing crisis won't just go away because of the council's financial position. My aim is to get everybody pulling in the same direction. It's not an option to hold our hands up and say we have no money.

In difficult economic times you have to make judgement calls. You have to decide which organisations add value to the community. What I'm looking for is a team dynamic that is evident when all sides of the partnership are trying to make Lewisham a decent place to live. I don't want voluntary groups to approach the council as a 'client'. When this happens I would say that the relationship is based on the voluntary group trimming its programme to fit the council's requirements because they need to get money out of the council. I want to see quite the opposite – voluntary and community groups that stick to their vision. Recognising each other's strengths and limitations is key. It helps if voluntary and community groups understand that I am a busy person and can't attend to everything or do everything. Street Pastors get that dead right.

Some of my colleagues start from the assumption that the council should do everything and control everything, but that's not my approach. Across the council there are colleagues who can become concerned because they think a street pastor will be a street preacher – they question the motives of faith-based groups. But in ten years of doing this job, I have met so many leaders of faith-based organisations who start the conversation with me by asking not what the council can do for them, but what they can do for the council. That's incredibly powerful. It really matters. And from then on I know we will have a positive discussion.

Street pastors asked very little of me. When they did ask, I did my best to deliver it. I was elected in May 2002 and it was in that first year, as I got to grips with the remit of the mayor, that I first heard about these people called 'street pastors'. Lewisham was, I believe, the third location that the initiative worked in. Our patch has several big nightclubs and pubs. You will see a lot of action in the area between the tube stations at New Cross and New Cross Gate with young people hanging out, traders feeling vulnerable, and sometimes drug dealing and robbery going on.

I was invited to meet some of the street pastors. Not my normal kind of meeting – this one took place at midnight. I found the notion of the scheme absolutely fascinating. Ordinary citizens from the ages of eighteen right up to eighty deciding to go out at night to chat to people with no agenda! In the middle of the day, in an unthreatening environment, we'd all like to think that we could do that, but midnight on the New Cross Road was not an unthreatening environment. I remember seeing a young girl sitting on the pavement, sobbing her heart out. It was a dreadfully vulnerable position to be in. There were big queues waiting to get in the clubs, and I saw how easily someone could become a sitting duck.

I encountered other characters who were around at that time of night, cab drivers and doormen. I realised that street pastors were part of a network. Until you see this network in action it is hard to understand. If street pastors were just good people, wanting to do good things, I don't think that on its own would work. They have to be known and valued; they have to share intelligence, by which I mean they have to keep channels of communication open and keep on breaking the ice.

So the council began to understand that street pastors were a fantastic resource and could be deployed in situations where policing and stewarding would only go so far. Street pastors could be successful precisely because they were not trying to police a situation.

What has surprised me most is how unlikely some of the volunteers are. There are lots of mums and senior women who are really well received by people on the streets, and they are effective in a way that many men are not. But these are not people you would expect to find on the street in the middle of the night in Deptford! Once you've opened your mind to the make-up of the volunteers, you realise it's all part of the story. If somebody has got something to offer, it's irrelevant what age they are, what their background is

Do I have any reservations about Street Pastors? No. From early on I was briefed that Street Pastors volunteers had to go through a structured training programme, and that each patrol would be made up of experienced leaders as well as newbies. I learned that they had already displayed a high level of commitment to get to the point at which they could go out on a patrol. I also knew that the police were supportive.

Street Pastors is an initiative that hinges on communities doing things for themselves. But remember, communities are not machines or faceless entities. They are made up of real people. Although we all benefit from the buzz around that word 'community', we can't write ourselves out of the picture and out of the work that needs to be done. And funnily enough, in all my meetings with faith-based groups, it's only been a street pastor who has asked me about my own beliefs.

FAQ

Don't street pastors just backfill the holes left by the cuts in local government budgets?

The question is really asking, where does responsibility fall for looking after those who need help in our society? Should we expect the government to look after us? As a Christian I would like to pose another question: do we believe in a sustainable community where individuals care for each other, where there is a 'thick' quality of inter-dependence rather than a faceless system at work? The opposite of social responsibility is consumerism which, in its purest form, sees everyone consuming based on personal choice and looking after themselves.

I believe that street pastors can complement local authority services, they can ease the pressure on hospital admissions and emergency treatment (and this does have an economic value). More than this, however, they are demonstrating that as human beings they take responsibility for other human beings. When we practise biblical compassion we are building a stronger society, regardless of deficits or credits in welfare spending.

Aran, church leader

8

The night I met a street pastor: Joanne

Joanne met street pastors on her last night out before undergoing gender realignment surgery. She tells how a chat and a cup of coffee with them made an impression on her.

Just to say, I enjoyed stopping for a coffee and chat last Saturday as I moved from one venue to the other. I stopped to show my support for the very worthy work that you do. So many people in today's society are too self-centred to help others! So by staying up late, often in the cold, to see a few people (often worse off for too much drink), well, it deserves a lot more respect and recognition than you probably get! So please pass on this email . . .

I look forward to seeing some of your members again when I'm next out on the town. I will stop to say 'Hi' and well done.

Joanne

'It was October and the weather was starting to get cold the night I first met the street pastors. I was going from one club to the next, with my party gear on. When I saw them, under a gazebo outside one of the churches in the town, I went over because I fancied a chat and wanted somewhere to stop after the hustle and bustle of the clubs. I had never noticed them before, but that's probably because I hadn't been out much because of my doctor's appointments and surgery and everything. I didn't know anything about these people, with their jackets and caps on, and my first reaction was surprise that they were staying up so late. I wondered if they would get proper thanks for helping others. That's why I wrote the email, I suppose.

'As I drank my coffee, I chatted with some of the street pastors. They made me feel very welcome. They asked how I was, where I was going that night. They were interested in me. They sat down with me. It was a lady and a gentleman, mainly, who talked to me. I felt like I was among friends. That was nice, really worth something to me, because I was used to a lot of grief from other people. Instead of feeling welcome I was used to feeling excluded.

'So I sat down for about twenty minutes, under the gazebo, with the street pastors. Our conversation was quite in-depth, not at all superficial. I know what it was that really struck me. Maybe it's just something peculiar to me, I don't know, but when I saw those street pastors it made me think about when I was a child and I had to go to church three times a day. I did it because my mum made me, but later I felt that going to church wasn't important any more. What was important was for me to follow my belief. For all this time I've felt that church hasn't kept up with modern life and it's only old people that believe in what the church stands for. And when I saw the street pastors, I thought, here's something different. It's the religious sector doing something in real life! The thing that I've always thought was just a shadow . . . there it was doing something real.

'My philosophy has always been "Treat others as you would like others to treat you." It's never had anything to do with Jesus. But I do believe in what Jesus stood for. I believe he stood for helping people, so it's better for me to help someone than it is for me to go to church. I was in Brighton last weekend and I met a girl with drink problems. She was homeless, too. I talked to her, showed her some respect, as I would like someone to do to me if I were in that position. So helping other people is more important to me than dressing up to go to church, and singing and praying.

'But, like I said, I don't always get treated as I would like. Over the last four years I've been living as a transwoman, going through lots of surgery and counselling, and feeling despair at the way I have destroyed the lives of my loved ones. When women talk about clothes, guys, going out, motherhood, I'm excluded from most of this. When I hear men talking I understand their conversations – I could join in with ease – but I've got no interest in doing that. I don't want to go back to that prison.

'So socialising is not easy for me, though I'm desperate for warm, caring friendship. I'm used to men greeting me with, "Alright, mate?" just to make sure I know that they know I'm a man. Going out takes a lot of courage, tolerance and diplomacy. I try to politely educate people into understanding this "gender dysphoria". Sometimes I've had to call the police to report a transphobic incident. The sadness of this has chipped away at my belief in humanity and I usually suffer serious depression for several days after an incident like this.

'Before I came here I lived in the Loire Valley region of France with my partner of thirteen years. Back then, as a man, I had my own business in haulage and plant hire. Really manly stuff! France was great. We didn't have to worry about locking the car, driving was easy, people weren't in a crazy hurry all the time. But it couldn't last and eventually I destroyed my partner's life as well as my own. When my mental health began to suffer, I couldn't get through the illness in France because my language skills weren't good enough. I took a couple of overdoses. My French GP said I needed to go home to get through the transition period.

'I had known from the age of eight or nine that I was different from other boys. In my twenties I got married, but that ended because I couldn't love my wife as a man (even though I still loved her deeply). In France I couldn't keep up the pretence any longer.

'I had no accommodation in the UK and so I had to check myself into the mental health system. After missing forty years of the basic contentment that most people have, I've been through seven operations and been living in supported accommodation for three years.

'Now that I've had my gender correction surgery, my hope for the future is that I will be loved and cared for because I am just me, fragile, vulnerable, loving and caring, but supportive, strong and reliable for others. The things I've been through, particularly my divorce and the breakdown of my second relationship, have really shaken me. For a while I lost my faith in being a good person. There was a backlash. I lost my faith in doing the right things – it was like being in a dark room. It's really hard to explain. Everybody learns a lot as they go through life, and some people have a religious faith that they can live by. I guess that's another reason I don't go to church – because if I did it would only be out of tradition; it wouldn't be to renew my faith. I live in this world. Although I believe that faith is important to human life, my mind isn't big enough to take in what faith might be like! I live in this world, with all its disappointments.

'Lots of pressures like the ones I've been through have taken people away from church. The way I see it is that church is a minor priority for most people. I think the church needs to move on, go out to people, not expect people to come to them. They ought to have a service outdoors in the park, so that everybody can see and hear what they're doing, and nobody would have to dress up. That's where the street pastors have hit the nail on the head. They're helping the church to step into people's lives. Like the Salvation Army at Christmas. People listen to them because they get out and about.

'My life is different from most people's. Apart from my history, I don't work so I don't have the same routines as other people. I have quite a few friends, but I'm not close to any of them. I'm a people person but I'm often on my own. I love the nightclubs, the liveliness, and seeing everyone enjoying themselves. The coffee the street pastors gave me that night was good. When I had rested my feet (in my high heels), I moved on before it was too late for free entry.'

9

Church off-centre: A re-positioning of spiritual engagement

....

Never underestimate the power of relationships! Through relationships we make the complex thing simple. We help each other to understand different views – worldviews and theological views. When we're actively developing relationships, our combined approach to challenges or opportunities is more robust than it would be otherwise. Ideas are more likely to be generated as more people gather around the table, and insights, expertise and experience can be shared. Differences in style between individuals can be enlightening and enriching. Each partner brings their strengths to the relationship. The increased capacity that working with others can bring may make an ambitious goal achievable. In terms of how a relational style of working is interpreted by others, it seems that the whole is always bigger than the sum of its parts, and can turn scepticism into interest, and change what once might have been viewed as a 'loose cannon' into a more cohesive, professional, credible unit.

In many sectors – education, industry, banking, the public sector – organisations and institutions have become aware that partnership can have a positive impact on regions and communities. As these institutions have played a part in the regeneration of the towns and cities in which they are located (through direct-action partnerships, through funding or research-based resources), they have realised their potential to influence for the better the life beyond their walls. Corporate Social Responsibility (CSR) has come out of the recognition that the activities of a large employer, manufacturer or service provider have an impact on the environment, on consumers, employees, communities and stakeholders. More and more we are seeing national and international brands attempting to enhance their public relations and connect with their customers by promoting their local 'face' and local 'personality'. To this end the new Tesco Extra store in Watford will contain a 'community space', a 600 square foot room that can be reserved free of charge and contains tea- and coffee-making facilities. Similarly, when a multinational bank gives floor space to a community choir on a busy Saturday morning, I see an 'overlap' between a big business and a small community group that makes me think that the global brand is actually interested in its local neighbours. It's good for business and a sign that new business models are appearing. Another example would be the food retail sector with its new resolve to bring 'life and colour' into the vast floor space of supermarkets (*Guardian*, 6 August 2013). Big high street names that would otherwise be homogeneous are acknowledging that they need to evolve to remain relevant, and with a local footprint and local partnerships they can spread economic and social well-being rather than keep it in one place.

This book has, I hope, something to say about the connections and the partnerships between the pillars of urban infrastructure, that 'urban trinity' of the police, the local authority and the Church. In this chapter I'd like to look at what the Church's own high street 'face' has meant for the reputation of Christianity in this country and how Street Pastors has changed that 'face', I believe, by practically demonstrating the gospel of Jesus and strengthening the public understanding of the *point* of Christianity.

The message and the method

The exercise of the message of the gospel in Britain in the eighteenth and early nineteenth century brought about the abolition of slavery, through the parliamentary campaigns of William Wilberforce, and protection for our society's most vulnerable people. After Wilberforce came Lord Shaftesbury, Elizabeth Fry and Thomas Barnardo, and many other evangelical Christians, whose political and cultural outlook was informed by their commitment to biblical principles. A glimpse of the vision for a new church under construction in the 1920s in Southampton, the Methodist Central Hall, is captured in a photograph of the half-built building, surrounded by billboards advertising plans for the church's function in the 'Docklands Settlement' and calling for 'Workers'. One sign read:

WORKERS WANTED
with grace, grit and gumption

Sick nursing among poor
Food depot and clinic
Maternity & baby care
Benevolent societies
Boys & girls Life Brigade
Legal advice bureau
Moral clinic
Evening classes
Organ recitals
Brass band and orchestra
Cast off clothing store
Children's play hour

How many of these roles or services do we recognise now, in the early twenty-first century, as within the remit of social and welfare services, the NHS or the education authority? This century-old snapshot of church engagement with society shows us the high bar that was set by, in this case, the Methodist Church, and how such provision from the faith sector devolved into state provision in later years. As the twentieth century progressed, the Church's social initiatives became less robust, with the missional message of social transformation relinquished in the shadow of the welfare state and government provision. In recent decades there has been an awakening to this segregation between Christian communities and the communities around them – communities shaped by politics, by geography, by history, by populations, schools and families – that has helped Christians to acknowledge that God's call upon their lives is to be integrated not isolated, to protect and bring flavour to society, to be beacons of light in the darkness (Jesus said his followers should be like 'salt and light'), and to believe wholeheartedly that he calls us to love the places where we live and have compassion for our neighbours.

As we read the wording on the Central Hall billboard we can recognise the emergence of this dynamic once again. Street Pastors, food banks and Christians Against Poverty (CAP) are examples of the work of Christian-led charities and the resurgence of this commitment to society. Some of the other services listed as part of the vision of Southampton's Central Hall – toddler groups, parenting classes, English language learning, and marriage preparation and enrichment courses – have consistently been founded and led by churches. Credible and professional interaction between a church and a community speaks volumes and open doors. The coordinators of Street Pastors in Southampton, for example, believe that the welcome that the Church has received in Southampton is jointly attributable to a 'history' of credible Church-led programmes in the city, such as Street Pastors, Southampton City Mission (SCM), and the establishment of two successful Oasis academies.

Through this work (in SCM's case for fifty years), they say, 'the city has seen that the Church can operate in unity and will do the things it says it will do'.

So what can we say about the withdrawal of churches from culture and society, whether that is in the past or today? Broadly speaking, Christian segregation happens when the Church begins to focus more on itself, on the upkeep of the building, on its own programmes and its own conventions. For the majority of the twentieth century, I would argue, the Church in Britain was devoted to maintaining the faith in this introverted way. The focus was on preaching the gospel rather than taking the holistic view that the kingdom of God about which the Bible teaches is concerned with empowering the whole person. I don't believe that the Church had totally given up its social vision at this time; it was happening (in the liberal wing of the British Church), but it wasn't having an effect on the visible face of the Church. By and large Christians were focused on making changes inside the Church so that people would come into it, rather than going outside the building to meet them.

This book is not a history of the British Church, nor can it trace in any adequate way the patterns of evangelicalism, mission and social action in this country over many years. But it can argue for the place of the Street Pastors initiative in debate about the way that Christians express their characteristics as followers of Jesus and offer to those around them the possibility of new life in Christ. Questions over the extent to which Church should engage with the world around it were influential until the 1980s and 1990s, and in some quarters today they define the emphases of a church's vision statement, its view of itself and its spoken and unspoken priorities. The ends of the spectrum are these: do we primarily make a difference through what we say – our public preaching of the gospel of Jesus Christ, or through what we do – the way that we engage with the world through our socially aware, gospel-inspired activity?

Although the Christian calling to exercise our responsibility to care for the world is laid down in the Bible, the 'turning outwards' that we've seen taking place in churches has been part of ongoing debates about Christian social action. I think there will always be some tension between those who believe that hope for mankind is best represented by the preaching of the gospel alone, and those who are committed to social action and whose emphasis is on the gospel having a tangible form so that people can feel it and see it. The Street Pastors movement has helped to crystallise the importance of applying and contextualising the Bible's message about a God who loves us enough to express his love on earth through Jesus.

How has Street Pastors focused minds on a holistic gospel? The original emphasis on the Church as *part* of urban power structures, not as aloof from them, was a new strand in the debate, and it was resisted by many of the church leaders that I spoke to in the early years of Street Pastors. The concept of working in conjunction with other secular organisations was not received positively by all denominations of the Church in Britain ten years ago, and I still find in some places that the commitment to preaching the gospel doesn't leave enough oxygen for the commitment to demonstrating it.

As we prepared to launch Street Pastors in 2002 and 2003, we came across a degree of uncertainty around the issue of churches collaborating with other non-Church agencies. I heard criticisms of the partnership concept, each comment varying slightly according to which denomination I was talking to. From the evangelical side of the British Church, I was told that Street Pastors 'polluted' Christianity and its partnership-based approach damaged Christian distinctiveness. I saw that some denominations were cautiously looking over the fence to see which churches were already involved and asking themselves, could they work with that particular denomination? To all of this I responded that Christians live with the challenge to be distinctively Christian in secular societies – to take responsibility for the world, but not become like it – to be 'in it' but not 'of it'. This is a relationship that has to be negotiated all the time, as we must stay alert to the dangers of compromise but be ready to get our hands dirty.

The turning outwards, whether in the Church or in other institutions, whether it happens smoothly or with a grating of cogs and wheels as the vast cruise liner changes direction, is starting to characterise the landscape of our towns, cities and institutions. At the same time that the Church's institutional status is weakening, it is also part of this increase in cross-community engagement. Of course, the Church has a unique calling to make itself known to the world, locally and globally; for each of its individual members to mature, discover and *re*discover the commission of Jesus Christ to 'go' to their neighbours and to all nations in the name of God. But what I want to stress is that through Street Pastors and other structures and projects like it, the Church now has a grass-roots activism that, like the high street bank hosting the community choir, is giving it a local 'face', a local personality and a local footprint. This is making it much easier for the general public to get hold of what the Church stands for.

Street Pastors has given the Church some credibility. The Church does a lot of fantastic work but its PR has let it down (in part, because Christians are always going to tend towards underselling rather than overselling). By making the Church visible and relevant to today's society, Street Pastors has enabled the general public to become far more aware of Christians as sacrificial and caring people. I'm sure that's why I've heard so much colourful language when people express their surprise at me being out on the streets in the early hours!

@MitchamChurches

Our 8 #StreetPastors out in a very cold #Mitcham last night came from 7 different local churches

The inter-church challenge

Alongside partnership with statutory bodies and the police, the second distinctive feature of Street Pastors that has affected the way that the Church is perceived by the general public is the stipulation that a Street Pastors 'area' is founded on the coming together of at least four different Christian denominations. Mobilising individual Christians to be, together, 'The Church', runs through everything that Ascension Trust and the Street Pastors network does. The idea that when you wear the Street Pastors uniform you are representing 'The Church', not 'My Church', is profound in its simplicity (vital to the general public) and profound in its doctrinal position (it says that followers of Jesus are united in heart and mind).

Street Pastors volunteers have become representatives of the Church and have reinvigorated an identity for the Church. Take, for example, a typical exchange between a street pastor and a member of the public. It goes something like this:

Member of the public: Who are you?
Street pastor: We're the Church.
Member of the public: Which church?
Street pastor: All of them.

Although street pastors have come out from the church building and bypassed its traditional daytime, Sunday routine, the dynamic relationship between the individual and the institution has been strengthened in two ways through the Street Pastors initiative: first, the movement has enabled the Church to play a bigger part in public life and, second, individual Christians have accepted their identity as part of the wider 'Church'. We know that, all too often, the Church's institutional identity has been expressed in negative terms (parochialism, sectarianism, competition), but the presence of Street Pastors in our towns and cities has aided society's willingness to recognise and use the simple label 'The Church'.

I believe that inter-church working is one of the principles that has enabled Street Pastors to grow into the diverse expression of Christians in action across the UK and beyond that we see today. It has been a principle that has encouraged the police and local authorities to support our work. It has been a principle that has made bigger and better resources available. It has been a principle that has helped Christians from different denominations be 'one in heart and mind' (Acts 4:32). It is a principle that has inspired churches to step forward at a time when the key players in towns and cities are looking for better integration with other civic organisations and want to explore valuable community resources.

Setting up the Street Pastors initiative ten years ago, I realised to a greater extent than I had before that there was fragmentation among churches and, in some places, a mistrust of ecumenism. In addition, people outside the Church perceived it to be divided. Our different denominations have created a sense for the non-Church person that religious folk have a variety of 'ways of doing things' and you need a particular skill set or knowledge base to be able to join in.

I believed then, and still do, that we needed to shake our priorities up. We need to hold less tightly to our theological views so that we are better able to look around us and see that our society is decaying, spiritually and morally. Scripture tells us that change will happen 'if my people, who are called by my name, will humble themselves and pray and seek my face . . . then I will heal their land' (2 Chronicles 7:14). Our priority should be, first, to bring a clear message about God's love and forgiveness and, second, to bring people together in order to make an impact as a missional group of people. We are then explaining and demonstrating the message of the gospel at the same time. Over the last century the general public has become well versed in what Christians are *against* and what we *disagree* with. We need to get a grasp on our public image again, make sure that we are creating positive stories for the news media rather than reacting to damaging ones all the time, and make it clear that we stand for justice, peace, forgiveness and reconciliation.

We won't overcome all of our divisions until Jesus returns. Theological and tradition-based alliances were around in Jesus' day (the Scribes and the Pharisees) and they are still with us today. I want to acknowledge that partnerships between Christian denominations that have been formed through Street Pastors are the work of God, not of man, so we are overcoming division in God's strength. Fragmentation is still a real issue, but we have seen a great move of God bringing people together and overcoming those differences.

@CaroSwannie
At @StreetPastors training an elderly lady asks: 'Can we hand out tracts?' The trainer's inspired response: 'No, YOU are the tract' #wisdom

Sometimes demographic development influences the level of unity or disunity between churches in a town, city or borough. Recent influxes, in the last twenty-five years, of minority groups into one London borough in the northeast of the capital have taken place at a pace too fast for successful integration between the minority groups and the established population. This has resulted in the white British community shrinking and the minority population creating its own strong communities, and these things combined have had a negative effect on churches in the area. There are now fewer churches, a handful with very large congregations and others that are struggling to stay viable, with a small and ageing membership. Asian, Polish and Tamil churches have become established and their desire is to serve their own communities. Although these churches are growing and have young congregations, integration and a city-wide focus is not something they are interested in. This history of churches not working well together, elderly congregations believing they have little to offer, large churches running their own programmes and ministries, and ethnic minority churches that are isolated, has meant that Street Pastors has found it difficult to recruit volunteers and gather inter-church, city-wide support. Out of eighty churches listed by a faith forum in this area, street pastors are drawn from only seven churches.

Sometimes the commitment of a church to its immediate locality means that its resources (human and financial) are focused on that environment. In large cities the 'city centre' may feel like a different place altogether and is thought to be a patch that is 'someone else's problem'. Coordinator of Newport Street Pastors, Les Tuckwell, identifies such a geographical gap in his city, and adds that it seems that some of the church congregations on the edges of the city are failing to realise that it's the people from the suburbs whom street pastors will meet in the centre on a Friday or Saturday night.

Ascension Trust has always articulated the fact that no single organisation can tackle the problems we face in the twenty-first century. No one church, no one department of social services. The first level of partnership that we look for is for churches to pray together, work together and overcome denominational differences together. They have to find a common ground (which I believe is the cross of Jesus), and start from there. Alongside expectations that Street Pastors teams are formed through partnership with local police and local government, is the requirement of Ascension Trust that a Street Pastors team is formed by a cross-denominational group of at least four churches. In the city of Reading, for example, fifty-two volunteers represent twenty-two churches.

Looking two ways

Street Pastors teams can find that they are in an important strategic position, able to look two ways – into the Church and out of it. Mandy Harding and Richard Pitt, coordinators of Street Pastors in Southampton, describe exactly this and believe that Street Pastors has stimulated relationships on both sides. 'We are comfortable with being interdenominational and working with secular partners. We are greasing the wheel for everybody else, we are bridging the gap, introducing our friends to our friends, drawing people together.' They describe an event 'a bit like a wedding' where they invited all sides of the family, churches, community groups and statutory bodies, during which a question was put to a diverse panel of people: 'What is your vision for the city?' At the time of writing, a city-wide initiative called 'Love Southampton' is currently under development as a result of that 'wedding', an open process involving a wide range of churches, Christian projects and skilled partners from local authority departments, such as fostering and adoption and youth services.

In this example, Street Pastors has initiated a flow of information between churches and 'the city'. I am grateful to God that the vision that he gave to me and the founding partners, for grass-roots engagement of Christians in their communities, partnership and interdenominationality, is becoming a platform that can take like-minded people inside and outside of the Christian faith, on to other, innovative forms of cooperation. I believe there is more to come.

The high street 'face' of the Church – the open door, the drop-in café, the parent and toddler group, the lunch for elderly folk, School Pastors, Street Pastors – has evolved as Christians have grasped their civic and Christian identity more strongly and with a sense that these two things go together, they don't pull apart. Christians have realised that there is something inherently 'civic' (belonging to a communal space) about their faith and, vice versa, they have realised that to be an active part of your community, to care what that place is like, is part of the expression of God's love for the world. I have seen a new awareness among Christians that what they have to offer their neighbourhood is of value not just to the 'user' (the person who will benefit) but also of value for the depth it adds to the quality of that community. I believe that this has meant that what Christians can offer has been articulated on a broader platform, with greater confidence, and confidence that has grown as our 'terms of reference' (what we will do and the way that we will do it) have got clearer and the invitation to us has been offered more readily.

I want to see Christians with a clearer sense of the holistic gospel that we believe in. I go to lots of meetings because I'm concerned about street lighting, education services, licensing hours, nightclub management and police priorities. I sit on different borough committees. I don't find many Christians at these meetings. Why? Perhaps they are at a church meeting. We need to pray, of course, but while we are praying, other people are discussing what our towns and cities are going to look like in fifteen years' time. Don't we need to engage with that? My faith leads me to keep abreast of changes in my locality, to stay informed and involved. I speak different languages: I sometimes speak in tongues but I can also speak the language of urban politics; I'm filled with the Holy Spirit but I have also educated myself about local strategies and policies. Don't mistake these characteristics for extremes – they are an expression of my God-given gifting and the holistic gospel of Jesus. The gospel of our Lord Jesus Christ reaches every part of society and every part that the natural man cannot reach.

Better public relations

I've always wanted to 'big the Church up'. In the first days of my life as a Christian I hunted for someone to take me to church, and when I got there I watched, bewildered but enthralled, as the building resounded with praise and hallelujahs. Since then I have made it my business to experience and take part in many different kinds of churches, humbly accepting the value of different traditions and passionately advocating the strength of working together. But the kingdom of God is people, not denominations, and I want to see more individuals committing their skills and their intellect to the work of the kingdom. I believe that many gifts and skills among God's people are lying dormant, and not enough of them are properly or adequately used. Any great thing that happens on earth – Street Pastors is a good example – is achieved not by one person, but by many, when different people with different gifts complement each other. In my preaching and teaching I encourage Christians to be part of this muscular body of the Church. We need to engage our minds and ask ourselves how we apply what the Bible teaches. Applied Theology is not just for Bible College, it's also for the place that we live in.

The Church needs to be reminded of its purpose and calling. 'We've got the whole Bible as our guide – we've got its sixty-six books,' I say to people, 'but it's still possible for the message of the Bible to be lost.' The word of God and the message of compassion, forgiveness and justice must motivate Christians. Even where the connection to the institution of the Church is weak or nonexistent and the struggle to forge a link with people is great, Christians need to be reminded that the word of God is alive and powerful.

Street pastors and school pastors are generally in contact with people whose connection to the Church is nil. They may be one or two generations removed from family members who did consider themselves a 'member' of a church. They may never have been inside a church building and may have no knowledge of what the Christian faith is all about. Despite the fact that there is usually a warm reception for the idea that street pastors do not represent a denomination but 'the Church', some street pastors find that the mention of 'Church' can bring a negative response, and so they bring the word cautiously into conversations. 'I find that saying that we are ambassadors for the Church,' says one volunteer, 'kicks the conversation off on the wrong foot. I prefer to sidestep the Church and communicate the fact that we are ambassadors for the good news of Jesus Christ.' Putting the name of Jesus into the appropriate places in conversation is the best way to take part in a spiritual conversation. The Bible tells us that there is power in the name of Jesus, and we must rely on that (Philippians 2:9–11; Acts 4:10–12). Yet although negative perceptions of the Church have grown up and the numbers of those who see themselves as belonging to a church are shrinking, neither of these circumstances mean that there is necessarily a corresponding lack of belief in God.

Informal spiritual engagement

Street pastors find that as they get well known on their high streets and outside the pubs and clubs they are accepted as people who inspire informal spiritual engagement. As sixteen-year-old Christi tells us in Chapter 11, she was able to talk freely to the street pastors that she met because she was in her own environment. She could enquire and ask the questions that were in the back of her mind without feeling intimidated and without having to commit to walking through a church door.

I estimate that 75 per cent of the people I meet when I am a street pastor ask me to pray for them. I think there are a few reasons for this. First, many people have a problem with the Church but very few people have a problem with Jesus. Second, becoming a Christian is the most exciting thing that has ever happened to me and I've had plenty of practice at communicating that excitement. I love to tell other people that if my life can be changed by God, then so can theirs. Third, street pastors care for people – following the example Jesus gives us – no matter what their lifestyle. Street pastors regularly get asked a number of questions, like: Who are you? What are you doing? Why are you doing it? Do you get paid? The answers to these questions help a person to understand that a street pastor cares for them, with no strings attached, even though they are a stranger. This often has the effect of encouraging an individual to open up.

People talk freely about their spiritual and emotional well-being with street pastors because they take us seriously. They know that we believe in what we are doing, that our faith is the reason we do what we do, and that faith leads us to sacrifice our own time and sleep to be with others. They see us as people of strong faith who won't point a finger. That all leads to them having the confidence to talk about their circumstances. It may be a question, for example, 'My nan has died, I don't know whether she has gone to heaven or hell', or 'My relationship is breaking up'. One night I came across a guy who talked to me for half an hour. At the end he simply said, 'Thanks for listening', and walked away. I had made that moment of vulnerability possible.

Other areas around the country keep their own statistical record of the types of conversations that they have with people. One such example is the city of Stirling in Scotland, where street pastors' monthly record sheets show that for the period March 2009 to March 2013, 8.1 per cent of conversations with the people that street pastors met on the streets of the city were of a spiritual nature. During this time the majority of these conversations took place with men (70.3 per cent). Men asked well over double the number of spiritual questions that women did and were twice as likely to be prayed for on the streets. The top five most frequently asked spiritual questions were about 'Jesus/God' (22.5 per cent), 'Church' (19.7 per cent), 'Faith' (19.3 per cent), 'Spiritual support' (prayer and compassion for difficult circumstances, 17.4 per cent) and 'the Bible' (10 per cent). (The

'Bible' category includes questions about a Bible verse or story and about the Bible's authenticity.) While 12.8 per cent of all the people met specified they had a church background, only 8.05 per cent had a current church connection.

In common with most Street Pastors teams, more than half of the people that the volunteers meet are aged eighteen to twenty-five, and while this demographic group may not be part of mainstream church, they are taking the opportunity to engage in spiritual conversations with street pastors. The reality is that the people we meet at 3.30 a.m. on a Sunday morning are very unlikely to get themselves into a church a few hours later. Street Pastors, although they operate in an after-hours vacuum, can be a link in the chain of an individual's spiritual journey as well as being an immediate source of practical care.

Frequently asked questions

The information drawn from the records kept by the coordinator of Stirling Street Pastors, James Mackenzie, shows that questions about 'death' and 'suffering' are consistently asked. Typical questions leading to a conversation about these topics might be, 'Why did my mum die?' and, 'If God is a God of love, why does he let earthquakes happen?' Another category 'type' relates to guilt. It might begin with a statement like this, 'My friend died in a car accident, and I survived.' Often there will be a question behind the question, so it's best to keep talking and try to uncover it. This may be particularly true of questions that arise from personal experience or anguish. It's not always possible to give definitive answers, and often definitive answers are (broadly) not helpful. Sometimes you will need to acknowledge that Christians hold a variety of views. Always ask what your questioner believes: 'What do you think?' and acknowledge their point of view.

I think the ability to respond to questions is a key part of a street pastor's role and the fact that so many people find us an accessible, approachable source of answers to deep questions or questions that relate to their experience of life and/or church (even in front of their mates) is an important dimension of our role. A member of the first group to go out onto the streets of Brixton, Sharon Constance, says that being a street pastor has developed her ability to open up her faith to discussion and questioning.

I didn't believe I had capacity to be a street pastor or answer people's questions. I couldn't always answer my own questions. At the beginning I wasn't sure that I would be a good representative. I'm grateful that these fears didn't stop me from going out. I realised that I just had to share what God had done for me. I believe my faith is what it is today because I'm a street pastor. It has made me more open, more able to discuss rather than enforce.

Some questions aim to trip you up. An example might be, 'Do you believe in dinosaurs?' In this case, try to discern whether the person you are speaking to is just baiting you and looking for an argument. Do they really care about what you are saying? As with all of the questions that street pastors get asked, ultimately it may not be what you say but the way that you say it (body language included) that they remember in the morning. It will be your love and care for them that makes an impression, not the finer points of your answer. In every circumstance, the street pastor's job is to be a great listener. We all tend to talk too much and we need to learn the skills of truly listening to what someone is saying so that we can 'listen' to the sense of self that they have. Someone who can engage with another person about their spiritual well-being, their bereavement, their anxiety, or the chaos in their life is someone who can enter another person's world without their own preconceived ideas.

It's vitally important that every Street Pastors team has prayer pastors who will pray for them, the people that they encounter and the events of each patrol. Penny Roe has been a prayer pastor for three years and she tells how praying with people from other Christian traditions has helped her to pray with more freedom.

When Street Pastors launched in my area I wanted to be one of the ones that went out on patrol, but I soon realised that my arthritic knee might slow the rest of the team down! To join the prayer pastors was just as big an adventure for me. I didn't know what to expect, but when the Lord leads us somewhere, we must trust him.

I approached prayer pastoring in trepidation. In my mind I equated praying 'all night' with praying in the dark, in the cold, with my hands gripped tightly together. The reality has been enlightening! We pray for the street pastors before they go out and they call in every fifteen minutes with reports about what they are doing and what we can be praying for. In the meantime we chat, but it's not just chatting. For me it's special because it's hearing other people's perspectives on churches and ministry in our area.

Far from being an uncomfortable experience, we love to provide refreshments for all of us in the team and we sometimes find that our table is literally groaning with food! It can be quite a social occasion.

Most of my fears came from the fact that before I became a prayer pastor I had hardly ever prayed out loud. I'm not a great one for public speaking. But as a prayer pastor I found I was among people who were quite happy to open their mouths and just pray. The mixture of traditions helped me to see that there is no strict formula to praying in a group. I heard some people praying so freely that it helped me to just open my mouth and speak what the Lord was bringing into my mind. Previously I would have analysed what I wanted to say until I completely lost confidence in saying it at all. I know this is also true for another prayer pastor who, before joining the team, had only prayed words that were in a prayer book.

I think I can pray with much more boldness now. We're all focused on the same thing, and I find the flow of information from the street pastors really useful, even if they are saying the town is quiet tonight. Somebody might pray for something that leads us onto something else. It's like throwing a stone into a pond – the prayers get wider.

FAQ

How long does it take to get a team of school pastors or street pastors set up and working?

I would argue that you can't 'parachute in' a team of school pastors or street pastors. Both initiatives have to work in a specific locality and that should be a locality where the ground has been prepared over years, not months or weeks. If you come and meet the team of school pastors that I lead, you will find that each of them has been building bridges into the community over a long period of time. Take June, for instance. She was a governor at the local school for ten years. If you want to demonstrate the fact that Christian people care for the community, one way of doing that is by building bridges of friendship – that may be through sharing fun times together or by working along-side others, by working together on plans and policies and by serving your community in whatever way God has equipped you. You have to be there for the long haul.

In my opinion, growing school pastors or street pastors from the ground up is the best way, so when we come to the table looking for an invitation to work with a school or a neighbourhood, the legwork should already be done. You are bringing a past reputation with you as much as you are promising something for the future.

Stuart, School Pastors team coordinator

PART FOUR

....

The Local Model

@Jack_Wakefield
Loved my night with street pastors . . . amazing seeing how when
Christians actually 'go', all denominations can work together

10

School Pastors:
Friendly adults for young people

A girl clings to the school gate, fearful of bullies. A boy writes a letter to his father, expressing himself like he never has before. Three young children skip along a busy road, unaware of the traffic. A school bus begins its journey, loaded with students and rivalries. A boy sits down in front of a computer game that will absorb him for the evening. A girl updates her profile on a social networking site, leaving herself vulnerable. In the shopping parade, antagonism grows with each day's influx of kids. A teenager, suddenly surrounded, knows his mobile phone has been taken. The classroom buzzes with talk of the riots on its doorstep.

These are just a few examples of the preoccupations and the pressures that some young people live with and that school pastors engage with. Although the issues that concern young people and the influences upon them are broadly the same whether they live in Torbay or Aberdeen, the educational contexts in which school pastors work and in which they are invited to participate, vary greatly. As a result school pastors take on a variety of roles, from patrolling outside the school to one-to-one mentoring inside the school. Their aim is to provide reassurance, safety and support to vulnerable children, in a compassionate and non-judgemental way. Their presence, which in some settings is very low key, expresses their availability as positive adult figures who will support students. I remember with fondness the lollipop man who would help me across the road on my way to school. I talked to him every morning for no other reason than that he was a friendly face. I believe that, as a baseline, we all need a spirit of friendliness towards young people and schools. The commitment of many Christians to their local school in a variety of settings around the country has shown that there is power in the simplicity of friendship.

What does a school pastor do?

The responsibilities of a school pastor are determined in discussion with the school where they will be working. Expectations and requirements in relation to school policies will also be tailored to the specific setting. The School Pastors website contains examples of the variety of roles that school pastors take. The core elements of the role are listed below. A school pastor will:

- Go on patrol at times and locations agreed by the school;
- Listen, be observant and look out for young people who are vulnerable, and respond accordingly;
- Build links with the school community, staff, parents, students, school crossing patrollers, etc.;
- Observe school pastor principles, health and safety guidelines and only work within the remit of the guidelines for the role of a school pastor;
- Take part in the school's own safeguarding training, if required (in addition to the School Pastors training programme);
- Be prayerfully aware of God's direction and share that with their team;
- Take part in other duties as requested by the school, such as mentoring or attending special events.

Timing

Earlier in this story, in Chapter 4 of this book, I tell how a meeting in 2002 with the borough commander for Lambeth, Chief Superintendent Dick Quinn, led those of us who had toured London, Birmingham and Manchester with the 'Guns on our streets' roadshow to the important discovery that the afternoon, between 2 p.m. and 6 p.m., was a critical time in terms of demands on policing. Between these hours, the chief superintendent told me, children and young people come out of school and college, levels of antisocial behaviour rise, and there is a perceived fear among adults with regard to young people, with the potential for antagonism to flare up between different sections of the community. All of these factors bring major challenges to the police. That is how I came to ask myself, how can we help to bring peace at this time of day?

The biggest challenge that I anticipated was finding volunteers who were available during the working day. I was right – it proved difficult. In 2002 the labour market was busy, businesses were doing well, and I knew that I would be fishing in a very small pool of labour. Though Street Pastors itself only started with eighteen volunteers, I couldn't bring together that number for School Pastors, try as I might.

Another obstacle was the reluctance of schools themselves to be creative in addressing the negative aspects of youth culture for fear of what it would do to their admission numbers and reputation. Many inner city schools were in denial about their students' involvement in violence or selling drugs, and were concerned about their reputation. They didn't want to do anything that would associate them with these problems, even though it was clear that some head teachers were aware that they were educating children who would, at some time, be involved with the criminal justice system. As we had already discovered through the roadshow and public meetings, the

167

police were still making efforts to keep sensitive problems under wraps, so there was little acceptance of the seriousness of the behaviour of young people and dangerous aspects of youth culture.

Then, as Chapter 4 shows, the problem of guns and gangs came out of the shadows with the shooting of four girls in Aston, Birmingham, on New Year's Eve, 2002. Sadly, there have been many violent and fatal incidents that have filled our newspapers and TV screens since then and the underworld of drugs, guns, knives and gang-related violence is now more widely discussed and exposed. I heard about the tragic events in Aston the same way as everyone else, on the TV and radio on 1 January 2003, and those events kick-started a new drive from the Metropolitan Police and from newspaper and TV reporters who were drawing Ascension Trust into public debate and comment. On top of this, I think that a new impetus was derived from the awareness that there was a massive vacuum where the response of the rest of the community to the problems afflicting some of its members should have been. Six weeks later we were training the first group of Street Pastors. School Pastors, which had not at that stage been strong enough to stand on its own two feet, was indefinitely postponed.

At that time I realised that Street Pastors could have more impact than School Pastors. What could be more dynamic than volunteers going out onto the streets at night just as other folk are locking their doors and tucking themselves into bed? My main aim hadn't changed: I wanted to be doing something. I wanted to invite others to join me and get churches mobilised to serve their needy communities. My vision for School Pastors was still strong, but the moment was ripe for Street Pastors. Three years down the line, in 2005, the Home Office came to Ascension Trust and invited us to start a pilot project in schools, and from this point on, we were active in working towards School Pastors. It took two years of talks with head teachers and local authorities, jumping through hoops and overcoming reservations, before we were able to launch the first pilot for School Pastors in St Joseph's School, Lewisham, south London, in February 2007. The initiative was formally commissioned in February 2011.

Other things have changed, too, in the years since 2002. As I've already inferred, schools have become readier to acknowledge that what goes on at home and in the community will have a bearing on what goes on inside the school buildings, whether that be family breakdown, inter-family feuds or cyber-bullying. This means that pastoral care is of increasing importance to the well-being of their students. In addition, in some areas schools know that the so-called 'postcode' rivalry between gangs may also be expressed in terms of rivalry between schools, leading to gang-related affiliations and violence. Strategies for early intervention are openly talked about and there is a willingness for schools to work with local authorities, police and voluntary groups to manage these problems and give added support to students.

Increased policing contact with schools is often delivered through Neighbourhood Policing Teams. Partnership work involving better information sharing and early action has also opened up schools to localised resources from a variety of agencies. Parents, teachers and local authorities have recognised the opportunity that such partnerships provide for engagement with young people. Nationally, over 450 Safer School Partnerships exist to help local agencies address behavioural and crime-related issues in and around a school. Schools have become a locus for partnership-working, as all partners have recognised that communities beyond the school gates can influence the well-being, safety and educational attainment of young people, for better or worse. As a Christian-led response to local needs, the School Pastors scheme has provided a structure through which churches and individuals can step into the new spaces that have opened up to play their part in the school community.

Though it can still be a struggle to find the volunteers to cover a daytime School Pastors shift, the increase in part-time working and, for some, the benefits of early retirement, mean that we have found that School Pastors schemes are now accelerating in numbers across the country. In most cases, School Pastors is being launched in towns and cities where Street Pastors is already operating (though this is not a requirement), and the credibility, professionalism and trust that Street Pastors has developed provides precious momentum for those Christians who want to demonstrate support for their local school and care for young people.

Grown from the Street Pastors platform

We had fantastic feedback from Street Pastors in Plymouth. I knew about their training, the high level of commitment that they have, evidenced in the fact that they pay for their own uniform. When we began to talk to the School Pastors team with a view to them working here at Plymstock School, I had confidence in them because of Street Pastors. I knew that they would not be pushing religion, though they are open about their ethos. I knew that, when they said that their job was to care for the students of this school, this is what they would do.

So says David Farmer, head teacher of Plymstock School, a large school with students aged between eleven and eighteen, in Plymstock, Devon, an independent town until it was incorporated into the city of Plymouth in the 1960s. School pastors patrol the grounds of the school and are present at the school gates one day a week, as students leave at the close of the school day. It easy to see that when over 1,750 young people leave the school premises at 3 p.m., it may not be an easy time for people who live locally. David Farmer stresses that it matters to the school *how* children leave at the end of the day when they spill out into the surrounding streets. As the students leave, members of staff take up positions on the exit route from the school, their rapport with the young people evident as they check that all ties are on and bikes are being pushed not ridden. They call out to individuals, 'We need to talk on Monday,' or laugh at a shared joke, 'I saw that photo of you and the cricket team!' The children reply or call out their own questions, but nobody stops walking. The tide of bodies keeps moving.

The head teacher's statement about working with School Pastors highlights two critical changes that have taken place for the School Pastors initiative since 2002 when it was first on the drawing board. First, over the intervening years, School Pastors has been able to draw on the success of Street Pastors. As David Farmer indicates, he, his school governors and senior staff were open to the possibility of inviting trained school pastors into the school community because Street Pastors in Plymouth (established in 2008) had already built a platform that positively shaped and influenced the perception of what School Pastors would be able to deliver. Second, the assumption that street pastors 'only go where there is trouble' at one time meant that schools were more inward looking and reluctant to involve school pastors in their pastoral care. Plymstock School was, on the contrary, happy to be associated with School Pastors; only for a moment, adds David, did they consider that questions might be asked locally about why the school and its students might need additional, supportive adults. 'Any uncertainty about our reputation did not last long. It's very rare for a school to get an offer of help like this. Giving their time for free, school pastors would help us to solve some issues in the support of vulnerable young people. They would be an extra layer of support.'

These two elements – the momentum gained through Street Pastors and the increased engagement between a school and the wider community – mean that in 2013 the School and College Pastors initiative is being welcomed into nineteen locations, with a projected thirty-five to forty by the end of 2014.

Young people, residents and retailers

The rest of this chapter will look at some of the ways that school pastors are building bridges with young people and at some of the elements that make up the relationship between young people and the wider community.

Late afternoon sees 85 per cent of Plymstock School's students making their way home on foot or by bike, many of them taking a route through the nearby shopping centre. 'After-school' time, therefore, is the sharp end of the relationship between the school and local residents and retailers. When Street Pastors was first discussed in Plymouth, a confederation of local retailers known as PARC (Plymouth Against Retail Crime) formed part of the planning group, in light of the fact that street pastors would be patrolling on their premises. PARC provided the Street Pastors teams with two-way radios and conducted training sessions with their CCTV staff. Later, when School Pastors was implemented, PARC gave £3,600 start-up money to School Pastors, with no strings. The school pastors have a base in the suite of rooms occupied by the shopping centre manager, and both sides are very supportive of each other's work and the new level of peacefulness that school pastors have brought to the town in after-school hours, a culture shift that is maintained even on the days when school pastors are not on patrol.

In a shopping centre in the northwest, the shopping centre manager describes how the retail outlets that he manages used to be plagued by antisocial behaviour (at all times of the day), with urinating in shop doorways, fights, and shoplifting on an industrial scale, with a fair amount of ill-feeling between young people and shoppers and vice versa. He comments that, unlike other, larger shopping centres, this one has no security guards and is not locked at night. 'Virtually all of the crime and anti-social behaviour has stopped since school pastors have been here,' he tells me. Looking around I see a bank of CCTV screens, thirty in all. 'The police used to be here all the time, but the only crime that we've had since Christmas is an elderly person being forced to withdraw money from a cashpoint for a bogus workman.'

The shopping centre manager, liaising between shopkeepers and the residents who live in the adjacent roads, has said to school pastors that he would like to see a chaplain in the area. He has observed the poverty of the residents (he describes them as poor financially, educationally and socially), and he has seen school pastors undertake the occasional pastoral home visit, caring for people by listening to what they have to say. As the School Pastors coordinator puts it, 'without truly understanding *how* we have made a difference with our one-day-a-week patrol, the shopping centre manager knows *why* we do it and that we have made a difference to the crime statistics and to people around here.' The coordinator continues, 'We don't have the power of enforcement or the power to change a person's finances, but we have the power of prayer.'

Orpington College in Kent was the first in the country to take the School Pastors model and apply it to the post-sixteen education sector. The entrance to the college is in a pedestrianised shopping precinct so, as with many other schools, the arrival and departure of students takes place within a 'communal' area. College pastors support the school's concern for the wider community, for the students themselves, and for peaceful relationships between different racial groups in the predominantly white British town, particularly at the end of the school day.

Young people and adults: Does anybody know what to do with teenagers?

Teenagers can be tricky. Until they get to know an adult they can come across as abrupt, dismissive and arrogant. Knowing someone brings more credibility to the interaction. Like all of us, young people get on a lot better when they know the adults around them and feel that, likewise, they are 'known'. Yet it is very easy for adults to feel intimidated by a group of young people. Adults can take an instant dislike to them; they automatically assume that they are up to no good, and then when negative words are said, the young people are not mature enough to ignore it, they react. As we say in the School Pastors training manual, 'Young people display negative input into their lives.' School Pastors have found that this particular culture clash is something they can speak about with integrity and authority. Many of them indicate that there is sometimes a need to educate other sectors of the community about how to cope with teenagers. Stuart Clarke, coordinator of Plymouth School Pastors, has often found himself brokering a better understanding between young people and adults. 'I say to young people, when you are in big group, some people are frightened, so cut down the language, cut down the volume, and things will be fine. To fearful adults I explain that the kids are just on their way home from school, they haven't done anything wrong, sometimes they like to show off.'

The ethos of School Pastors makes a difference to the interaction between adults and young people, says Stuart, because instead of isolating teenagers, our relationship with them – as 'friendly adults' who are not teachers or parents – helps them to see that they are part of something bigger . . . the community. As head teacher David Farmer puts it, 'School pastors in my school are a community looking after a community.'

School Pastors in Southampton tell how they came across a

group of children who had fallen out. They spent a few minutes with them, helping to restore calm, and as they walked away they bumped into an elderly couple walking their dog and stopped to chat. Noticing the dog, the now peaceful children came over and made a fuss of it. 'We left them there together, the elderly couple who would often complain about the behaviour of young people, and the young people who wouldn't find many opportunities for positive interaction with adults outside their family.' It's an example of how School Pastors can build bridges between different parts of the community.

A presence ministry

'Some days we have nothing to do; the report card that we use to record incidents, conversations and prayer requests has nothing on it. What we do conclude from that?' asks Stuart Clarke of his School Pastors team. As this chapter makes clear, school pastors take a variety of roles, according to local needs and the invitation that the school gives them. Some, who offer a calm, neutral presence at the school gates, may worry that it may look as if they are not 'active' enough. The term 'presence ministry' is used by Stuart to describe the work that school pastors do in Plymouth as a way of drawing out what is purposeful and God-inspired about their role, even on quiet days.

A school pastor can be a reassuring presence for young people by simply exchanging a few words with the students. Those who are vulnerable, or who struggle with peer-to-peer relationships, may forge stronger bonds with the volunteers. Teachers at a secondary school in Southampton value the adult–child interaction that school pastors initiate, saying that time spent on the computer or in front of the television at home means that some children spend very little time speaking to adults and the low level of speaking and listening skills has a negative effect on a child's literacy. Meeting a school pastor provides a child with an opportunity to talk to an interested adult.

Well-developed lines of communication between a school and school pastors enable school staff to follow up on any incidents or issues brought to their attention quickly and appropriately. Ruth Evans, head teacher at Cantell School in Southampton, says that, when communication is established like this, 'our capacity to support and care for all our students is increased, and for this reason we think school pastors are fantastic.'

School pastors need the same observational skills that street pastors develop. In Southampton, school pastors noticed three young children, the oldest of whom was about seven, making their way to school unaccompanied. The oldest child was listening to music on her phone and her two younger brothers were skipping on and off the pavement, unaware of the traffic around them. The school pastors followed them down the road to make sure they were all right. The next day, when they saw the children again, making their way to school in exactly the same way, they knew that they really needed to make contact with the children. They phoned the prayer team and then continued to follow the little group. Turning a corner the school pastors found that the children had stopped because the youngest child's shoelace had come undone and the other two kids didn't know how to tie it up. The school pastors were able to ask their names, give them some help and take them into school where they drew the teacher's attention to the children's lack of road sense.

When a school pastor is 'present' amid the crowds going home after school, they are a presence that is known and respected. They are valued because they practise what they believe as Christians and because they uphold a non-judgemental code. So there is something 'active' going on in the recognition that they receive from teachers, parents, local residents and students. What Stuart describes as the right 'attitude of approach' always requires prayerfulness, empathy and openness, and we know that those things are not always our default position, but are characteristics that we choose intentionally by asking God to grow and inspire them in us. We know that, through prayer, a Christian is never inactive. Remember, the small team of ten school pastors in Plymouth, with its one-day-a-week patrol and its 'quiet' days, is the same team that has been instrumental in deterring '99 per cent' of antisocial incidents and criminal behaviour in the shopping centre near the school!

'I believe that we "preach" with every footprint,' says Stuart, 'and that through us God's light is brought into darkness.' There are moments when, Stuart says, the pastors in Plymouth know clearly 'that they have done something', when they are reminded of their purpose, and feel that they are more than a presence. One such occasion was the day that they found a young girl clinging to the gateposts at the entrance to the school, unable to get herself home or go back into school.

I enquired if there was anything we could do to help. She poured out her story, how she was being bullied on the way to school and at school, and was terrified that it would happen on the way home. The school was aware of the problem and was taking measures to resolve it, but in her words, 'they can't be everywhere'.

We said, 'Would it help if we walked you home?' She replied that she would like that. After phoning the girl's mum to ask if it was OK for us to walk her daughter home, we walked with her, saw her up the garden path and waited for her to wave from the front window to let us know she was safe.

We met the girl and her mum in the shopping centre later and Mum thanked us. Over the next six months we prayed for the girl (anonymously) with our prayer pastors. Then, one sunny day, when the grounds were full of students having lessons outside, we came across the girl with her teacher, and the teacher said to me, 'This girl has changed in the last six months beyond all recognition.' The girl herself then turned to me and said, 'It's finished, it's all over,

I'm safe again.' Her ability and her desire to work at school had also improved beyond recognition.

On the day that school pastors walked this girl to her home, they made a point of telling a PCSO who was walking through the area what they had done, in case the officer received any reports of school pastors walking away from school with a child. 'As I explained everything to the officer,' continues Stuart, 'he hung his head and stared at the ground. When I finished speaking I asked him what was wrong. Mumbling, he told me that *he* too had been bullied at school. Here was a guy in his forties for whom bullying was not yet resolved.'

School pastors were able to help ease the problem of bullying for the girl and, although the solution was not immediate, they were resolute in praying for her. This is an example of the partnership they have with the school: the school were doing what they could in the environment over which they had juris-diction, and we did what we could outside the school gates. It is an informal partnership, and if it had been formalised it would probably not have been as well accepted by the girl. They were able to provide reassurance to the girl because, to use a term used in the evaluation report of the launch of the School Pastors scheme at Archbishop Tenison's School in 2008, they are accepted as 'capable guardians' with a non-divisive approach to adults and young people.

Gaining depth and breadth

The partnerships that school pastors initiate are expressions of early and informal intervention. They are often examples of a diversionary approach. In several settings, school pastors are involved in pastoral care and mentoring inside the school, for example in Religious Education lessons and assemblies. In Aberdeen, they take part in life coaching sessions for students.

Southampton School Pastors support the Year Six transition into secondary school; they have a whole week of mornings and afternoons at the secondary school and the feeder school, and are then available during the first week of term at the secondary school.

In Newcastle school pastors spend time getting to know the students informally during lunchtimes. Volunteers travel on the local service bus with students into Byker and the city centre. This gives them opportunities to get to know the main instigators of antisocial behaviour as well as the more vulnerable young people. At the end of this chapter you can read about Newcastle School Pastors' 'prayer space', set up in Walker Technology College.

At Archbishop Tenison's School in the borough of Lambeth, relations with the school have steadily matured, and volunteers now work with children who have been temporarily excluded from classes. When school pastors arrive at the busy boys' school at lunchtime, they chat to teachers to see how the day is progressing and who they might need to spend time with. At 2 p.m., when afternoon lessons begin, they will take a group of boys, sometimes as many as eight or nine, into the room set aside for school pastors. Here the three regular volunteers will listen and chat to the boys, who might need to talk about things going on at home or personal difficulties. Sometimes school pastors challenge their patterns of thinking or discuss with them the consequences of their behaviour.

Team leader Neil Charlton says that the boys clearly understand that school pastors are not teachers or parents, and that anything they say to them will be kept confidential, as long as it isn't going to harm that individual or anyone else. 'They often tell us important information that couldn't be shared in any other context.' He lists communication skills as one of the biggest needs of these teenagers, together with issues arising from missing fathers and wrong ideas about masculinity. 'We never underestimate the value of listening, allowing someone to be completely open, and being open and honest ourselves in return,' says Neil. 'We try not to rush in with solutions. Many of these young people are facing complex situations and we need to have a good understanding of youth culture, and where they are coming from.'

Be encouraged and challenged about the ways that you can serve your school community. 'Intervention' is many things but for school pastors it begins with the Christian community helping to support another community and providing another layer of support to young people.

A school in Newcastle invited school pastors to temporarily convert the school library into a prayer space. Anne Fothergill explains the idea behind giving young people a physical space in which to investigate prayer.

When we said 'Welcome to our prayer space', some of the students looked at the floor, some folded their arms, some tutted. There were a few volunteers who were happy to put their hand up to say that they knew what prayer was, although there weren't many who said that they did pray. It's not a cool thing to do for most young people. They did listen intently to our explanation of what the prayer space meant. It was certainly different to their perceptions of church – an old building tucked away in the corner of the community, mainly for old folk, only open on a Sunday morning. If you went to church you had to pray with your hands together and eyes closed, they said. Or you might kneel down.

If we don't offer young people the chance to experience communication with God, how will they ever learn another view of the Christian faith? The prayer space gives schoolchildren freedom to explore what prayer means. The freedom is important because they spend a large part of their day being told what to do, how to do it and when to do it. Through a prayer space we want to make them a simple offer – the offer of an opportunity to choose to communicate with God.

We asked the school if we could set up a prayer space, and when the time came for them to refurbish the school library they offered us the use of that room for a week before they got to work on it. So we set up the prayer 'stations' (areas), and added some low lighting and background music. Our prayer space had seven creative, practical and interactive areas based on topics such as feeling sorry, forgiving other people, letting go (asking God to carry their worries and fears). There was a large white board on which students could graffiti their own prayers and a world wall covered in maps and issues currently in the news, plus an area on the village in Kenya that the school supports. There was also a 'Be still' gazebo for those who wanted to simply be quiet and still.

The prayer space gave students ideas about how they could engage with God. The choices they have – to move between the different areas, to wait and see, to observe, or to interact – reflect the choice that we all have to engage with God.

The students reacted very well to it. Those that had shown in their demeanour as we welcomed them that they didn't think much of the idea hung back for a while. A percentage of young people went straight into the activities while others stayed in the middle of the room, within reach of everything but not making a move to one area in particular. In the end there wasn't one person who didn't engage with it. We didn't cajole them to join in and we made sure that the teachers didn't do that either. We made it clear to the students that there were no expectations on them in the prayer space and there were no time limits. We simply wanted to offer them the chance to reflect and to feel a sense of freedom instead of restriction in the context of communicating with God.

In the introductory time we asked, what is prayer? What do you know about it? Have you experienced prayer? We explained that it is a conversation between us and God, and there are different ways of offering our prayers to God. God answers prayer in different ways, we told them, and sometimes he doesn't answer in the way we would expect or sometimes we have to wait for an answer. We were keen to get across the idea that this wasn't a magic wand exercise, but if they truly wanted to engage with God he would be faithful.

We were struck by the outpouring of grief and loss that was expressed on the white board. This wasn't only the loss of grandparents, but siblings, cousins, aunties. Since the prayer space week, the head teacher has said that he recognises the need for students to have a more permanent 'outlet' like the prayer space, and so in the next academic year we will be setting up our own School Pastors room in the school where students can come for an informal chat. We want to be trustworthy adults to them and through our care for them to offer them broad and open opportunities to ask questions and understand something of God.

FAQ

If Street Pastors is so great, why can't you open it up to people without a Christian faith?

I've had the occasional meeting with individual councillors who ask this question. My answer goes something like this. Let's assume that we would want to do that – to invite non-Christians to train to be street pastors. Whose rights are we going to take away to make that happen? The person without a Christian faith who doesn't want to pray or read the Bible when we train? Or would it mean a restriction on the rights of Christians who want to pray about what they do? Christians get their strength and courage from Jesus. I don't want to take that away from them. That's the reason we do what we do as Street Pastors volunteers. It doesn't stop us from welcoming the chance to work with people of another faith or no faith who want to set up similar initiatives. We are not exclusive, but we want to make our own contribution.

Mark, Street Pastors team coordinator

11

The night I met a street pastor: Christi

....

Christi first came across street pastors in her home town when she was celebrating her sixteenth birthday. She explains how they have watched out for her and drawn her away from trouble when fights and arguments are all around.

'I like going out in a big group. Sometimes my nights are quite quiet, other times there might be fighting. When people go out and have a few drinks, they get really outspoken, don't they? They are more sensitive than they would usually be and even the smallest things have a massive impact. It can be so easy to get into arguments, especially in the town I live in, where everyone knows everyone else.

'When I first met the street pastors I was only sixteen and I was out celebrating my birthday. They were a bit concerned for me because I told them I was used to staying out late. We got talking and they asked me if I would like to help make food for the street pastors when they came back from being on shift. That was their way of giving me an alternative to being out on the streets so late at night, and they thought it would also be something proactive and positive for me to do. I don't think I was ready to change at that time and I carried on staying out late with my friends.

'Street pastors are really good at calming things down. I've seen them stop things that would have escalated into something much worse. With me and my friends they would often try to distract us and they would get me to come and stand with them so that I was out of the way of trouble. I've never been angry towards street pastors as they have always had a calming influence. I've always had lots of good conversations with them, sometimes about alcohol. They've told me I don't need it to have a good time.

'There was one time that I remember them particularly looking after me. I like everyone to be happy and so I tend to jump in when things are kicking off because I want everyone to calm down. This time I was trying to split up two girls who were fighting and I got dragged around by my hair and bashed against a car. The street pastors stayed with me and kept me warm – my friends were drunk so they were no use. The street pastors put me in an ambulance. Since then they have specially watched out for me; they encourage me to stand with them, and give me reassurance.

'Right from the start I was friendly with one of the street pastors because she was my teacher at school and helped and supported me through school. She introduced me to her sister who is the wife of the pastor at my church, and her parents, who are both street pastors. I had no knowledge of what it meant to be a Christian but I knew enough to worry that the street pastors might judge me because I was doing things that were against their faith. I have never felt judged by them, though. Mainly I was curious about what they believed. I would often argue against it. I would say, "But how did this happen? How is this true?" We talked about the way that God wants people to be. One of the street pastors told me to stop trying to answer my own questions. He said, "Just let God answer them." I found that difficult because I'm the kind of person that likes to find the answers, but what he said really stuck with me.

'I eventually started a discipleship course. I didn't think I would be a believer, I was just curious. I started going to church and my church has always been really supportive of me. I'd been going there for a year when, one morning, as I was talking to someone, I began to feel a presence around me. I hadn't been happy for a long time, but then, right at that moment, I felt happy. I got baptised in May 2012. It has been a long journey because of my non-Christian background, but I'm learning and slowly getting there.

'Meeting street pastors helped me on my journey to being Christian. What really made an impression on me was hearing the street pastors speak about their own stories, and the ways that they had come to know God. Some of them, like me, come from a family or a life that wasn't Christian. They told me that they were normal people who believe Jesus died for them. It baffled me, but when I was with them it was easy to talk freely about it because I was in my own environment.

'I'd like to say that I'm really thankful for the ongoing support I get from the street pastors, and each and every one of them should be extremely proud of the work they do – I know it has had a huge impact on the crime rate in the town and the attitude people have towards Christians. The time that they give and their dedication doesn't go unnoticed.'

12

The Street Pastors network

....

When Street Pastors started it was an informal, church-based response and its unexpectedly fast growth has posed a lot of challenges. At the outset the edges of the initiative were a little bit fuzzy; Ascension Trust started out 'doing' Street Pastors itself and in the early years we had to urgently think about what the relationship between the administrative hub and the dispersed local teams should be. We didn't have the capacity to run Street Pastors in a growing number of areas, so we asked ourselves, what is the best role for us? What was needed was an understanding of how a Street Pastors area (a team in a given town or city) would relate to Ascension Trust. Our answer was that governance and quality control was the role that we should take in relation to individual areas around the country. We had not anticipated the dramatic growth that we were seeing which was, at times, overwhelming. The trustees of Ascension Trust and I would laugh about how we could not keep up with God: 'Can we slow this thing down?' we said!

As we have worked to define our responsibilities and those of the local teams, we have needed to accept the shift in language and terminology that it has brought. In short, Street Pastors is not one charity, but a network of independent charities in the UK and overseas.

The importance of a strong structure at the local level

The Street Pastors initiative is all about encouraging the local church to be a presence in its community to care, listen and help. The vision for Street Pastors is that in any local area, volunteers can come from any denomination or background; the initiative is not owned by any one church or tradition. In order to have that strong relationship, we have found it works better for these relationships to be built up locally; we would find this difficult to do from London. We don't have the local relationships or the understanding of the history of churches, key players in the local economy, or a knowledge of police and community relations in a given locality. Local people – people who know what is expected of them and are able to engage in local relationships and encourage others to be involved – are the basis of the strongest model for Street Pastors. We are committed to ongoing, long-term ministry, not short-term solutions.

In some cases the extent of this independence has not always been fully grasped. As we have developed the language of 'network' and got more explicit about it, some teams have been less keen, or less quick to grasp what it means for them. Ascension Trust is an umbrella organisation, working in partnership with local charities to deliver Street Pastors in a local area. We are ultimately responsible, but the local area (and its trustees) is responsible for what happens locally.

@Jane_Flynn
#streetpastors odd night. Found a wandering elderly lady. Went with her and police to A&E and ended up there all night. So sad. So lovely.

How do we ensure excellence among the network?

Sustaining quality in the context of local variations is a vital part of Ascension Trust's work, and you can learn more about this from our Legal and Policy Adviser, Andrew MacKay, later in this chapter. When a Street Pastors charity is going through the setting-up process, Ascension Trust provides a great deal of help and guidance. We have a Trustee and Coordinator Pack, with a large range of documents, materials, policies and procedures, covering, for example, governance, finance, patrolling procedures, how best to work with volunteers and general best practice. We continually review our documents, to make sure that we can best serve the charities through the information that we send out. We also regularly send out information and updated materials, to ensure our charities are kept abreast of the latest guidance. It is so important that our Street Pastors charities have the tools to be able to run Street Pastors themselves, excellently and locally.

But we are also committed to supporting our local Street Pastors charities as much as they need. We provide ongoing help in a large number of areas, from supplying high-quality uniforms, to delivering training, and providing help on legal, financial and operational questions. We also provide more in-depth assistance where necessary. For example, we have worked with a group of Street Pastors teams in the north of England, talking through with them the pros and cons of different models of joint working to find a solution that works for them. In the southwest of England, we have also provided help to a Street Pastors charity that was going through difficulties with governance and the relationships between staff and trustees. We helped them understand their legal obligations and best practice for trustees, employees and governance, encouraging them to review how they work with employees.

Every two years we also have a quality assurance process,

which covers each different area of operation of the local charities. Quality assurance is a tool to help local trustees and staff address structures that they might not have put into place, or strengthen areas where they might be weak; from Ascension Trust's side of the relationship, it helps us identify areas where local charities are struggling, and we can bring assistance or guidance to those groups where necessary.

How can Ascension Trust best serve its charities?

We spend a lot of time thinking through what are the best resources that we can put into the hands of our charities. This will range from training and Internet resources through to information about policies and improvements in Street Pastors merchandise. We consider and respond to requests for items with Street Pastors branding, such as umbrellas, flip-flops, mugs, pens or bags. Some of these items are useful for fundraising. We want to be able to be competent in organising the things that should be in the background, so that street pastors and their management committees can better get on with putting into practice the vision that God has given them.

Our central aim is to give local teams confidence to be effective in their context, not to micromanage them. Our start-up pack and online materials are an important way of devolving some of this responsibility. In more complex cases, our Ascension Trust representatives (ATRs) will work with an individual charity to help them learn from situations or think an issue through. We want all our management teams to grow in wisdom and experience as they apply their own judgement to the basic principles of operating Street Pastors where they live.

We are also available to help all street pastors position themselves correctly in relation to the legal principles that underpin many of the situations they encounter. In the second part of this chapter, Andrew MacKay gives a few examples of how

Ascension Trust, local trustees and individual street pastors have needed to fully understand how the law is worked out in practice in a particular circumstance. A delicate blend of our pastoral role and our role in respect of the law and policing is sometimes required.

These are some of the ways that we work behind the scenes to keep the network running smoothly for the independent Street Pastors charities that we work with. If you are interested in investigating whether the place where you live could launch a Street Pastors initiative, take a look at the next section.

How can we set up a new area?

A new Street Pastors area usually starts with a local person expressing an interest in bringing Street Pastors to their town or city. That person (or group of people) will then establish that this interest is shared among several local churches and that there is potential for significant partnership between them. These steps are outlined on the Street Pastors website and an email address and phone number can be found online so that you can make contact with Ascension Trust once you have started this process and formed an alliance of interdenominational churches.

The next step is normally for a representative of Ascension Trust to visit your area and share the vision for Street Pastors with you and answer your questions. If, after prayer and discussion, the core team of people that you have gathered together feel that God is saying 'Yes' to the initiative, the next stage is for a Licence Agreement to be signed between Ascension Trust and the new area. The Licence Agreement is a document containing the understanding and expectations in terms of our relationship with an area, signed by each management committee at the outset of our partnership. It outlines the way that the relationship will work and defines the commitments that Ascension Trust makes to local teams. From here we will take an area through several more stages of preparation before a new team is launched.

What does a strong and sustainable Street Pastors team look like?

- It has enough volunteers to ensure that there is minimal disruption when someone is ill or unable to carry out their shift (i.e. the weekly rota doesn't use everyone to their full capacity);
- It is a team where individual street pastors are flexible and happy to patrol under different team leaders;
- It has a desire to share resources between neighbouring teams, e.g. training sessions, prayer pastors, socialising together;
- It has good leadership: team leaders and management committees who consult with their teams, communicate well, give feedback, and make sure there are opportunities for everyone to contribute;
- The team develops good relationships with local police and establishes good patterns of briefing from duty officers on each patrol night;
- It balances experienced team members with newer ones;
- It plans ahead to keep a flow of new recruits. They might lead a presentation to churches in their area once a year, or print flyers or 'business cards' to promote their role;
- It knows that observation is often a good entry point for those who are 'just looking' or dipping their toes in the water. It can also provide the opportunity for those interested in being a prayer pastor to get a taster by

being an observer for a few hours one evening;

- It proves its strength as a team by occasionally encouraging team members to swap roles: inviting prayer pastors to go on patrol as observers and street pastors to pray for the night;
- It is a team that ensures that training is refreshed when appropriate, and especially, the 'Roles and responsibilities' element every three years;
- It is a team that spends social time together.

The international picture

In the context of the growth of Street Pastors overseas, I often get asked, 'Are you building an empire?' The question comes from cynicism about the motivations for development and expansion. In answer I always remind the questioner of Jesus' great commission to his followers. 'Therefore go and make disciples of all nations . . .' (Matthew 28:19). We at Ascension Trust believe that, under the authority of Jesus, this applies to us, as it does to all Christians, but that we are not the best people to shape and deliver the Street Pastors initiative on the ground in each city or country. We believe that it is, therefore, our responsibility to work with those that approach us, to communicate the vision to them, encourage them to pray, give them a structure for discussion and make sure there is a clear grasp of expectations on both sides. Our desire, in obedience to the commission of Jesus Christ, is to give our structures to a local area for them to use appropriately in their local context. Beyond the first areas – Lambeth, Hackney, Lewisham, Birmingham, Manchester – where we were aware of the massive need for street pastors, we have never instigated the initiative in an area. There are over 270 teams across the UK today because people have come to us to start the setting-up process.

Ten years ago, when we shared our embryonic ideas about the initiative with church leaders, police officers and local government officials from London boroughs, we heard them say, 'Don't do it, it won't work.' When we added that we believed the way to bring this idea to life was to reach across church denominations and draw Christians together, they said more loudly, 'It won't work.' But it did work because it was God's agenda. So the bottom line is that Ascension Trust has a can-do mentality, not because we believe we are great, but because we believe if we stick close to God, he will do what looks humanly impossible.

We have already seen spontaneous growth in Street Pastors areas as individuals move from one city in the UK to another and take their experience of Street Pastors with them. Recently, two volunteers from Shrewsbury who have decided to emigrate to New Zealand asked us how they can promote Street Pastors in their adopted homeland. Our strategy is for the good news to reach people's ears organically. It is best for people to see for themselves and get a taste of what street pastors do, and then make their own enquiry. This way we find we are able to travel with them without any suspicion of our motives. In addition, whenever the movement hits the news we get an upsurge of interest around the world.

It is a great delight to us at Ascension Trust that we are starting to see that Street Pastors can be a passport to interaction between Christians and communities all over the UK and beyond. Our training is our gold standard. We take the training of new and existing street pastors very seriously and we believe that once a volunteer is trained they are 'available' to any town or city because they carry their experience with them. All they will need to transfer from one Street Pastors area to another is an understanding of the local scene. The training that one person does in Telford is essentially the same as another person does in Gibraltar. This potential for the identity of Street Pastors to be recognised across the world excites us. One young man travelling in Australia, whose parents are street pastors in a town in the southwest, is an example of how this universality can be perceived. Feeling unsettled, a strong sense that he had to talk to someone came over this young man. God was prompting him. He knew that a team of street pastors had been launched in Manly, near Sydney, and he searched them out. When he located the team he was able to talk to them and, during his stay in the area, he gave his life to Christ. Even though he was far from home, he knew that street pastors were the people he could go to!

With the exception of Trinidad and Tobago, and Chico, California, volunteers in countries outside the UK will wear the same Street Pastors uniform. (The colour of our jacket was too close to the police uniform in Trinidad and Tobago and so volunteers on the islands wear a sky blue jacket. In Chico the polo shirt is a different colour because, again, the original colour was thought to be too close in colour to the police uniform.)

Our first challenge at Ascension Trust was to build a network and an organisation that could respond to the phenomenal growth of the movement. Now, in the second phase of our operational life, we know that the challenge facing us is to ensure that, with over 270 individual charities across the UK and the world, we protect the Street Pastors name and secure quality control. It is part of our stewardship of Street Pastors to make sure that all our charities are operating to specified standards. The Street Pastors logo and name must be protected in order that the public can have confidence that anyone in a Street Pastors uniform is working closely with Ascension Trust and conducting themselves to a high standard.

Street pastors are beneficiaries of the reputation that the organisation has built up over ten years, and they have a responsibility for its upkeep, making sure that they don't jeopardise it in any way. We do our best to enable them to do that with our support and expertise. As with all successful Christian movements, we are always watched closely and we must be ready for that close scrutiny and accountability.

The table below shows where (outside the UK) Street Pastors teams have been set up or are in the process of being set up at the time of writing.

Country/state	Area	How did Street Pastors get here?	Status
Antigua and Barbuda	St John's (capital city)	The vision for Street Pastors was communicated on one of Les Isaac's annual visits	Teams started operating in 2008, coordinated by overseas mission workers, Paula and Martin Callam
Australia	Manly, Sydney	Brett Mitchell, a Salvation Army officer enquired about Street Pastors when he became a member of a committee of local church representatives tasked with responding to the outcry from the Manly community about antisocial behaviour in the business and commercial district of the city	Discussions began in 2009, with the official launch on 1 May 2010

California (USA)	Chico	A mention of Glasgow Street Pastors in a book encouraged an enquiry to Ascension Trust	Training started in May 2013
Maine (USA)	Bangor	Renee Garrett, a street pastor in the UK with connections to Maine, opened discussions with Ascension Trust	Conversations between church and community leaders and Ascension Trust started in February 2013
Eire	Cork	Initial interest was generated by Street Pastors trainer, Simon Thomas	Trainees were commissioned in July 2012
Gibraltar		Fidel Patron, who became coordinator of the Gibraltar team, heard about Street Pastors at a Methodist conference in the UK	Trainees were commissioned in March 2012

Jamaica		The vision for Street Pastors was communicated via Les Isaac on one of his annual visits to the Caribbean	The initial inspiration for Street Pastors came in 2003 and relationships with Jamaican pastors have been ongoing. Training is due to start in November 2013
Nigeria	Badagry	Rebecca Gbededo, a street pastor living in Eastbourne, made the link between Ascension Trust and churches in Badagry, the birthplace of Christianity in Nigeria	The first approach to Ascension Trust was made in 2012. The discussion is ongoing
Trinidad and Tobago	Tunapuna	Penny Carballo-Smith and Lehoma Tannis Harriet introduced Street Pastors to Trinidadians. A delegation visited London to observe street pastors in action in July 2010	The first patrol took place in March 2012

Andrew MacKay is a solicitor who works for Ascension Trust as Legal and Policy Adviser. He provides expert support for street pastors, coordinators and management teams, often in relation to drugs, assaults, safeguarding of children and vulnerable adults, media relations and insurance.

I worked as a commercial solicitor in Scotland before moving to London to get married and take up a post in an American law firm in the City. After some time I found that the long hours and the lifestyle were overly draining, and I decided to move on, first to work with the Lawyers' Christian Fellowship and then to the role of Legal and Policy Adviser at Ascension Trust. I had been attracted by the work of Street Pastors for several years and my church is very supportive of it. I was (and still am) excited about being able to use my legal skills in a way that makes a difference for God's kingdom.

If you've read anything else in this book you will know the 'heart' that is behind what street pastors do. My job, along with the rest of the Ascension Trust team, is to be a good steward of the expression of care and concern that is that 'heart'. We recognise that it is important to look after, protect and provide resources for the Street Pastors volunteers and movement that God has entrusted us with. I feel this responsibility, and I am increasingly trying to remember that Street Pastors is not ours; we are holding it on trust from God. In the story Jesus told, known as the parable of the talents, the master commended his servants for putting his money to work while he was away, so that they could ultimately repay more to their master than they were initially given. We need to do all that we can to ensure that we are wise stewards of God's resources and that nothing detracts from the honour and the blessing that God has given us in Street Pastors. It is my desire to use all that God has given me to honour the reputation that Street Pastors has.

I am a commercial litigation lawyer by background so I am used to the challenge of having to understand a wide variety of relevant laws and how they might take effect. In the Street Pastors context, this means understanding the important areas and principles of law, how they affect the Street Pastors charities and volunteers, and what is best practice for the good governance, leadership and management of charities. It is my job to make sure that behind the scenes, all these policies and procedures are as tight as possible. My hope is that as few people as possible know about what I do, so that these things are not impacting the work of street pastors on the street!

It is also my role to ask the difficult questions and address situations that must be tackled. While I can sometimes slip into 'lawyer' mode, I have learned a lot from Les Isaac and Eustace Constance and the way that they place such a high priority on people and relationships. I watch them engaging with the people behind the question or the issue and, in the same way, I don't just want to treat people simply as 'clients'. I can be task-oriented, and I'm aware of the pressure to let the relational side of my work slip, but I try to find a balance between providing answers to difficult questions and responding to the people behind the enquiry.

There are occasions when I need to take time over a phone call or a meeting in order to make sure that someone is properly supported as well as giving them the right advice. I recently took a phone call from the chairperson of a Street Pastors charity who, in his full-time job, was facing a challenging financial situation that had led him to seek advice from Christians Against Poverty (CAP), and had eventually meant that he had to declare himself bankrupt. This person had phoned me to ask what the implications were for his position as chair. The Charity Commission guidance is that this gentleman is not entitled to remain a charity trustee and so he is in the process of resigning and looking for a replacement. As you can imagine, this was a sensitive conversation, and I wanted to ensure that the man and his family were coping with the situation as well as simply providing advice. That same balance between pastoral care and getting the details right applies as much to me at my desk as it does for a street pastor out on patrol.

One way we try to support our Street Pastors network is by

providing all the materials they might need, in the Trustee and Coordinator Pack. It contains a number of suggested policies, covering health and safety, data protection, safeguarding vulnerable people, and equal opportunities. Very often there will be questions about how these things are worked out in practice. It's important to make sure that all Street Pastors teams are legally compliant, that the best policies and procedures are in place, and that local teams can get advice about any difficult legal questions and situations, because there are many complex legal questions that street pastors may encounter during a patrol.

Perhaps an example will help. Imagine a team of street pastors out on patrol who come across a young girl, who appears to be under sixteen, who claims to have been sexually assaulted. They are faced with many questions: how should they best deal with the girl? Should they tell her parents? Should they inform the police? How can they ensure that nobody in the general public is negatively affected by this incident? In a case like this you can see that street pastors must find a way forward that does not compromise the trust they have built up between themselves and the local community but, at the same time, make sure that they do not obstruct a criminal investigation.

Safeguarding is an important area of the law, and there are strict guidelines for working with people who are vulnerable. That's very relevant to street pastors. We need to make sure that our volunteers don't harm each other or the public, either unintentionally or intentionally.

These are some of the tensions that individual street pastors volunteers face and that we try to help with; on the one hand street pastors are a reassuring presence when they go out; they engage with people who are living antisocial lives, who may be, for example, dealing drugs or working as a prostitute. Street pastors connect with people like this; that is the pastoral element of Street Pastors at work. But on the other hand, one of the major benefits that Street Pastors teams frequently see is that they are able to contribute to a reduction in crime. So, clearly, there can be a tension between wanting to be a pastoral presence for an individual but, equally, not wanting to hinder the police.

To help keep the right balance, we have worked extensively with the Metropolitan Police to produce an agreement between the police and street pastors in London, which has also been used as a model for other police areas around the country. The purpose of the agreement is to ensure that police and street pastors know how the relationship between them will work, and that is important for our volunteers. We have agreed that, generally, street pastors will not get involved with low-level incidents of criminal behaviour, possession of drugs, antisocial behaviour etc., that they come into contact with or hear about in the course of their patrols. If the police are looking for witnesses to low-level incidents, they should not be asking our street pastors, because they have other means at their disposal, such as CCTV. In the case of a serious incident, the police are able to ask the local coordinators for a statement from street pastors who were witnesses. It is really important that our street pastors are seen as trustworthy. Although street pastors encourage people to uphold the law, we want pastoral care to be the primary role that is in evidence in local communities.

FAQ

Does the work of Street Pastors stop a person from realising the consequences of their own behaviour?

As Street Pastors we aim to help, to listen and to care for people with the love of Jesus. Matthew 7:12 exhorts us: 'Do to others what you would have them do to you, for this sums up the Law and the Prophets.'

When people go out and get drunk, I don't believe they

plan the evening thinking that if they get themselves into a vulnerable state, street pastors will sort them out, just as they don't think about other possible consequences of drinking too much, such as getting arrested or finishing their evening in the A&E department. People are people and will not always make wise choices, and our role is not to judge but to be there for those that need us. We do receive numerous emails and phone calls of thanks from people we have helped, and some encouragingly tell us they will not be repeating their actions of the previous weekend!

It could be argued that in preventing some hospital admissions and arrests, street pastors stop people from facing the consequences of their own behaviour; or it could be argued that through responding to their need we honour the command of Jesus to love our neighbour as ourselves.

Joy, Street Pastors team coordinator

Afterword

....

It was 3.30 a.m. and I was in a nightclub, a fat spliff smoking in my hand. I heard a voice beside me. 'You don't belong here,' it said. The music was loud but I heard that voice quite clearly and knew it was God speaking to me. The surprise for me was not just that he spoke, but that he was there, in that club. In the weeks that followed I toyed with this oddity, this rearrangement of expectations. 'What was God doing in that nightclub?' I kept asking. The answer I arrived at was that he was looking for me. Simple as it was, my question and my answer grew in meaning over the years. They started to tell me something even more profound – that God is not limited like us. He is on the move, surprising us.

I hope this book has shown you something of the movement of God through Street Pastors. I say to God now, just as I did when the initiative was in its infancy, 'Do something by your Spirit, God, because there are many obstacles in this path.' I believe that God has raised me up, and brought others alongside, for the task of managing and stewarding the grass-roots, spontaneous growth that he has given through Street Pastors. Other street initiatives have come out of it, and we thank the Lord for them. Ten years ago, I would not have believed that Street Pastors would be what it is today. When we smell success, or start crunching impressive numbers, people tend to comment, 'Your PR is great.' I say, 'This is not PR. This is God.'

The 'story so far' is important because it reminds me of the hurdles that the organisation has overcome and, at the same time, focuses me on the ways that God is continuing to move through Street Pastors, and the new shapes that are unfolding.

As an organisation that mobilises thousands of people who help others stay safe in the night-time economy, Ascension Trust is pleased to be opening discussions with the alcohol retail industry. Our common goal is that towns and cities should be welcoming places at night. Supermarket chain ASDA has begun to champion our work and is keen to establish links between each of their stores and the local Street Pastors team, making local teams the in-store charity and enabling shoppers to support the work of their street pastors. In Chico, California, street pastors went out on patrol for the first time this year. What will the movement look like in the USA in another year's time? Street Pastors is currently being introduced into church life in Nigeria and we wait to see what kind of impact the initiative will have in Africa.

I believe there is more to come. Join with me in thanking our God of new beginnings for his moving, creating impulse (Isaiah 43:19), and the next time that you meet one, thank a street pastor for all that they do.

Useful addresses

Ascension Trust
www.ascensiontrust.org.uk
info@ascensiontrust.org.uk
Ascension Trust, Alpha House, Alpha Place, 158 Garth Road,
Morden, Surrey, SM4 4TQ
Tel. 020 8330 2809

Ascension Trust Scotland
www.scotland.ascensiontrust.org.uk/contact-us/
scotlandenquiries@ascensiontrust.org.uk
Suite 4D, Kinnoull House, Friarton Road, Perth, PH2 8DG
Tel. 01738 248143

Street Pastors
www.streetpastors.co.uk
info@streetpastors.org.uk

Street Pastor (new area) enquiries
newarea@streetpastors.org.uk

School Pastors
www.schoolpastors.org.uk

National Prayer Pastors
prayer2@streetpastors.org.uk

Word4Weapons
www.word4weapons.co.uk

Prayer Spaces in Schools
www.prayerspacesinschools.com

Christian Police Association
www.cpauk.net

Purple Flag
www.atcm.org/programmes/purple_flag/

Christians in Parliament
www.christiansinparliament.org.uk/publications